HOLDING CHANGE

**THE WAY OF EMERGENT STRATEGY
FACILITATION AND MEDIATION**

adrienne maree brown

Praise for *Holding Change*:

"adrienne maree brown is powerful both as a healer and as a thought leader. Her revelatory work, *Holding Change*, arrives at the intersection of activism and whole-wellness, at a time when the world needs it most. *Holding Change* is about improved communication, achieving conflict resolution, and making space for others while still holding one's self in high regard. A necessary and mighty tool."

—**Patrisse Khan Cullors, co-founder of Black Lives Matter and *New York Times* bestselling co-author of *When They Call You a Terrorist***

"adrienne maree brown is not an outsider looking into movement work but a weaver who has committed her life to our collective liberation … She helped us advance our structure, systems, and vision in ways that allowed us to stay grounded in our north star. She is a master adapter and a gift to the movement."

—**Karissa Lewis, Rising Majority**

"Adrienne is the most powerful, insightful facilitator I have ever had the privilege to witness, let alone work with … Her technique is a powerful demonstration of how strong, innovative facilitation has the ability to help leaders build visionary movements."

—**Thenjiwe McHarris, Blackbird and Movement for Black Lives**

Holding Change: *The Way of Emergent Strategy Facilitation and Mediation*
Emergent Strategy Series No. 4
© 2021 adrienne maree brown

This edition © AK Press

ISBN: 978-1-84935-418-9
E-ISBN: 978-1-84935-419-6
Library of Congress Control Number: 2020946122

AK Press   AK Press
370 Ryan Avenue #100   33 Tower St.
Chico, CA 95973   Edinburgh EH6 7BN
USA   Scotland
www.akpress.org   www.akuk.com
akpress@akpress.org   akuk@akpress.org

Please contact us to request the latest AK Press distribution catalog, which features books, pamphlets, zines, and stylish apparel published and/or distributed by AK Press. Alternatively, visit our websites for the complete catalog, latest news, and secure ordering.

Cover design by Herb Thornby
Printed in the United States of America on acid-free paper

CONTENTS

Author's Note

There are a number of ways to work with this book. All of them begin with the Foreword and Opening.

1. You can continue reading the book in order, front to back.

2. Or, after the Opening, you can do the Assessments and let the results guide you to necessary parts of Facilitation and Mediation, and then come back to finish in the realm of Black Feminist Wisdom.

3. Or, after the Opening, you can read all the Black Feminist Wisdom and then move into the skill areas.

4. After the Opening, you can read all the Mediation sections first, then Facilitation, then Black Feminist Wisdoms, and then do assessments as you pivot to application of the lessons.

5. Or, you can read the book oracle style, opening to a page or part at random and letting it guide the facilitation or mediation of the day.

Foreword

My body of work is mostly about attention. I want to bring my attention, movement attention, and the flow of our human attention to the places we as a species most need to learn and grow.

With *How to Get Stupid White Men Out of Office* (2004), the focus was: how do we practice complex strategy that advances our organizing work while also harnessing our power to contend for electoral territory?

With *Octavia's Brood* (2015), the focus was: how do we attend to, and liberate, imagination, recognizing that we must imagine what we want to create as a future society; imagine who we need to be in order to move and grow in life-affirming directions; and imagine solutions, even when we are told we have reached an impossible problem or condition?

With *Emergent Strategy* (2017), the focus was: how do we attend to being part of the living world? How do we learn from nature, from the constant force and beauty and power of this planet, and how do we partner with change?

With *Pleasure Activism* (2019), the focus was: how do we attend to, and reclaim, pleasure, satisfaction, and joy, in and as the work of justice and liberation?

With *We Will Not Cancel Us* (2020), the focus was: how do we attend to the ways we treat each other within movement, and how do we cultivate an abolitionist attention for humans who make mistakes?

Now, with this book, the focus is: how do we attend to our collectivity in ways that align with nature, with pleasure, with our best imagining of our future, that support the ways we contend for power, that support our visionary abolitionist movements? Which is to say, how do we attend to generating the ease necessary to help us move through the inevitable struggles of life and change? How do we practice the art of holding others without losing ourselves?

This book is about attending to coordination, to conflict, to being humans in authentic and functional relationship with each other—not as a constant ongoing state, but rather a magnificent, mysterious ever-evolving dynamic in which we must involve ourselves, shape ourselves and each other.

Thank you for bringing your attention to this work.

Opening

Holding Space, Holding Change

Welcome to this offering on holding space, or holding change, which can also be spoken of as the sacred way of facilitation and mediation. This is the Opening, and it is my intention in these first pages to give you everything you need to most effectively use this book.

Holding change is a variation of holding space. I use it to distinguish my use from others,[1] but also to foreground that this is the emergent strategy approach to holding collective work, and emergent strategy understands that all is change. Space is never fixed by literal, physical dimensions. It varies according to histories, dynamics, emotional nuances, moods, pressures. It does change. It is change. We hold space for each other to change at the individual and collective level. I will use the terms interchangeably throughout this text.

You picked up this book because you hold space for others, and want to weave your ways and these ways into something exquisite.

Or you got this book because you want to hold change, and hold it well.

Or...maybe you're just like, what exactly is holding change?

---

1. Particularly at this moment in movement, I want to hold the distinction between what I offer here and the incredible facilitation teaching that Autumn Brown and Maryse Mitchell-Brody have been growing in the Allied Media Conference space for years in workshops titled *Holding Space*.

Do you remember being young, guided in an exercise of breathing where you cupped your hands around an invisible ball of energy and moved it?[2]

Breathe with me now, either visualizing or practicing:

In front of you is a ball of energy. It is yours, an extension of you. It hovers in the air, shifting with your attention.

Breathe out while pushing this invisible ball of energy away from you.

Breathe in, bringing the energy into and all around you.

Breathe out, move it up above your head, spreading it into a massive glorious umbrella.

Breathe in, bring it back to center and hold it there.

Breathe out and take it down through your bones to the floor.

Breathe in, rolling back up and bring the energy back into your heart.

Keep breathing.

Whenever I breathe this deeply with others, I feel calm, I feel how solid this presence, this energy, is, in me, in my hands…even when I am time traveling from the moment of me writing this to the moment of your reading it.

Since I was young, in most rooms, I could sense the tangible—the demographics, the looks on people's faces, the body language, the excitement or exhaustion. But I could also—can also—feel the room, feel the matrix of the intangible, invisible, the space between the bodies, the space that is fed by our collective emotion. It feels thick and vibrant to me, nearly solid at times.

Do you feel it?

It has taken me a long time to understand all the things I feel, all the feelings that are possible. Sometimes, there are thrills up and across the top of my spine and shoulders. Or a trembling in my gut. Or deep roots extending down from my hands and feet, growing wide under the room.

I used to try and deny these feelings.

---

2. I later experienced this flow as an adult in tai chi and qi gong practice.

Then I tried to control them.

Then I began to study feeling.

I became fascinated that not only can I feel so much—but that all of us have the potential to feel the space we can't see.

Now, I've spent years learning how to facilitate and mediate using both the things I can see and the things I can feel to guide my moves. I started hearing the phrase "holding space," and it felt like a beautiful way to understand and express what I was up to. Later, as I integrated that change is the only constant, I came to understand my work as holding space for change, holding a space in which change is inevitable.

So. What is holding change?

To "hold change" or "hold space" is to hold both the people in, and the dynamic energy of, a room, a space, a meeting, an organization, a movement.

To hold change is to make it easy for people with shared intentions to be around each other and move towards their vision and values (facilitate), and/or to navigate conflict in a way that is generative and accountable (mediate). I will dive more deeply into what facilitation and mediation are in those sections, but the basic definitions to grasp here are that facilitation is making it as easy as possible for groups of people to do the hard work of dreaming, planning, visioning, and organizing together; and mediation is supporting people when conflicts or misunderstandings arise that make it hard for them to hear and understand each other in direct conversation.

Holding change is something I have learned with and from so many cofacilitators, especially a generation of humble and dynamic Black feminists, so this book weaves my lessons together with wisdom from other Black feminist facilitators.

I am most experienced in holding change for people who are trying to change the world and generate justice and liberation, primarily with Black organizers, feminists, and climate warriors. Most of the lessons and reflections I will share in these pages were learned from holding space for movement workers focused on

Black liberation and climate justice, though I am blessed to have been in service to many movements of my time, including reproductive justice, HIV/AIDS, and antiwar.

Holding change happens in a number of different ways:

I have facilitated groups in a service-provision way, where they hired me to help them move towards their predetermined goals.

I have facilitated groups in experimental ways, where I supported them to show up, trust each other, and let the direction emerge, often pointing towards healing organizational trauma, shifting structures, and clarifying vision.

I have facilitated groups coming into existence, and groups that were complete and ready to sunset their formation.

I have facilitated groups that have claimed success, and groups that have felt like they failed.

I have mediated people in formal (not legally mandated) ways—where I was asked to set up a specific time and process to help people move through conflict.

I have mediated (much more often) conflict that has come up in the midst of a gathering and needed to be held and moved through to attend to the group's continuation of their work.

I have supported others as a doula, holding space for birth to unfold in miraculous ways, towards death, towards life. Ah—there is nothing like being with the instant and total devotion of new life coming into existence. A new organization, movement formation, or idea can sometimes have that same miraculous energy. The doula sensibility now shows up in every part of my life and I wish more people in our culture had a root system in some lineage of powerful care.

I have mediated movement workers through romantic and friendship and organizational breakups.

I have held the hands of friends and strangers going through loss, death, grief, broken hearts, lost pregnancies, failure—quiet space, screaming space, impossible space. Space filled with tears and longing. Space where we faced, together, that which is perpetually unfair and mysterious. Space where we learned what shapes us and what would make us strong.

All of this holding has shaped me. We don't always know all the ways we learn to facilitate, but it helps me to consider that every part of my life is shaping every part of my life, every experience shaping me. On this journey, teachers are everywhere, in our own thoughts and actions and in every interaction and mass action.

Other facilitators have been a gift to my life and learning. Many of these facilitators have very different perspectives on the work and call of facilitation than I do. Some tilt more towards outcomes, others more towards process, or logic, or fairness, or magic, or planning.

This is a time when we need a lot of facilitators and mediators—a lot of holders of change. We are at a very particular moment in human history, a period of time when we need to shift away from the competitive, directive, combative, colonial energy of toxic leadership at every level of society. The structures built to pierce the sky, the walls conjured to make the earth a puzzle of combating territories, keeping some in power and others without it…all of these structures are crumbling.

It is time to move towards ways of being that are focused on listening to each other deeply and accepting each other, whole. We need to learn ways of being in space together that help us see beyond false constructs of superiority and inferiority without asking us to sacrifice what has shaped us. We need to study being receptive and nonjudgmental with each other, letting the earth and community hold us until we remember we already belong.

I believe holding change can be sacred work, and I'll admit it is most satisfying to me when the sacred is palpable in the room.

The lineage of holding space reaches back to our original ways of being in relationship with each other and the earth. Like many displaced peoples, I have had to find my way back to listening to the earth and my own nature through longing and intuition, gathering little pieces and practices, studying different methodologies, asking a lot of questions, stumbling, making mistakes. I am still returning.

With time, some of the indigenous roots and paths of these practices and methodologies have been revealed to me. I believe that even if I can't see the roots, they are there. I believe that anything new I feel myself innovating is an adaptation of something that came before me. Circles talking, doulas holding, humans releasing tension, heartache, vision. It excites me that over and over, humans have realized that some of us can support others in this way, some of us are called to hold the containers in which life transforms and the future unfolds. As always, I will try to walk the line of honoring complex lineages of this art, this science, these methods—while accepting the mystery and apparent randomness of my own learning.

There is a simplicity to facilitation and mediation—holding, listening, reflecting, deep breaths, yes, say the truth, find the way forward.

There's also a remarkable complexity to this work. Humans are complex in every way—structurally, spiritually, emotionally—we are constantly changing into something else. Emergent strategy is about helping us find our place in this complex existence, perhaps even making it simple to be complex together.

I won't presume to tell you everything about how everyone should facilitate and mediate. I am not focusing here on tools you can find elsewhere—I am offering what feels fundamental to me to share right now for those who want to bring emergent strategy into their work of facilitation and mediation. Most of this book is about how to be and think in the work of holding others through change. Of course, in my heart of hearts, I believe this is the way, and this way would serve any who truly tried it on. All of this is invitation, and if at times it is proselytizing invitation, forgive me, and see me.

The Spirit, The Way

The spirit of this book is to offer up everything I know about facilitation and mediation, as simply as possible.

There are so many people already practicing emergent strategy facilitation and mediation—if that's you, please take from this text as it's useful. Add your own notes all over it.

If you are just beginning your journey with emergent strategy, there's a refresher in the next section, but I recommend reading *Emergent Strategy: Shaping Change, Changing Worlds* before diving in deep.

It's taken me a while to relax into the idea that, after more than twenty years of holding change, I have some things to share. Things that are bigger than me. The concepts of emergent strategy predate me—I believe they were gifted to us for this time and generate a stronger bond between our species and this planet, and each other.

I want the concepts and growing practices of emergent strategy to be available to anyone doing movement work, and to anyone who wants to learn from, partner with, and even surrender to being part of the natural operating systems of the world. I believe that if you listen to the natural world, you will inevitably find your place in movements for social and environmental justice.

The words in these pages are things I've learned and offered while giving facilitation trainings, spoken in speeches, things I have woken up knowing, dreamed, caught in a candid conversation. Things I have jotted down while facilitating groups. Things about facilitation as a practice and instinct, things I am not convinced can be communicated in words, but which I really want to share.

I have been deeply moved by the *Tao te Ching*, the work of a Chinese philosopher named Lao Tzu, translated many times in many ways. It is full of brief lessons that inform a way of moving people and power, understanding the forces of the universe. One of my very favorite stanzas of the *Tao* is:

> the tao (way) that can be spoken (named, told) is not the constant (eternal) way.
>
> the name that can be named is not the constant (eternal) name.
>
> the nameless (unnameable) is the beginning of heaven and earth (the eternally real);
>
> the named (naming) is the mother (origin) of all (particular) things.

Every time I write to capture a way of understanding or doing anything, I am instantly humbled. I am trying to describe something that I am feeling, learning, something unfolding, something changing, that has a million paths, of which I may only grasp one.

And there are things that are true about facilitation and mediation that I may not be able to put into words, or may never be able to make clear.

The facilitation I most love feels like a sacred act. In addition to the strength of a good agenda, clear direction, generative agreements, and values-aligned logistics, I believe facilitators offer our most powerful contribution when we operate from faith—faith that this work in this moment will shape change. That the people in this room are a collective succession of Harriet Tubman, Frederick Douglass, John Brown, Grace Lee Boggs, and other known and unknown freedom fighters.

As facilitators we step back from the knowing that makes us stand out as individuals, the call to make ourselves distinct from each other and the universe. Facilitation is a commitment to the power of the collective. We hold space for humans to find each other, clearing the debris between them so that they can access the forward motion of life, the flowing river of change, the rich ecosystem of differences.

There are moments in facilitation when you can feel the way to the future unblock, when you can feel the room burst forward on behalf of the species. In those moments, I can feel the tingling prickling aliveness of interconnection, of history, of futures becoming possible. Even in those moments, looking around at each other all brightly shining with the present moment, there are no words vast and timeless enough for the spirit amongst us.

So in the humbling impossibility of eternal communication, I name facilitation and mediation as ways the spirit moves towards justice! I weave myself into the lineage of understanding facilitation and mediation as a way we bend the arc.[3]

Emergent Strategy Refresher

Emergent Strategy is fundamentally about how we get in right relationship with change, realigning with an indigenous worldview that understands the relationality of all things. At the intersection

---

3. "We shall overcome because the arc of the moral universe is long but it bends toward justice." —Dr. Martin Luther King Jr., "Remaining Awake Through a Great Revolution," Speech given at the National Cathedral, March 31, 1968.

of ancient understanding, science, the sacred, and science fiction sits a set of principles that helps us practice shaping change.

Nick Obolensky defines emergence as "the way complex systems and patterns arise out of a multiplicity of relatively simple interactions."[4] Emergent strategy is about how we shape and generate complex systems and patterns through our own relatively simple interactions. Nature moves in small fractals of interdependence, accumulating nonlinear changes and creating more possibilities with the constant adaptations of a resilient earth. If we attend to nature's lessons, we can remember that we, too, are nature; we can unveil our own organic gifts, our way to the future together, our path to thriving in this abundant world. Emergent strategy invites us to give up competing for death and begin collaborating with the planet and each other towards life.

Octavia Butler	(amb)
All successful life is	(Fractal)
Adaptable,	(Adaptive)
Opportunistic,	(Nonlinear/Iterative)
Tenacious,	(Resilient/Transformative Justice)
Interconnected, and	(Interdependent/Decentralized)
Fecund.	(Creates More Possibilities)
Understand this.	(Scholarship, Reflection)
Use it.	(Practice/Experiment)
Shape God.	(Intention)

4. Nick Obolensky, *Complex Adaptive Leadership: Embracing Paradox and Uncertainty* (Burlington, VT: Gower, 2014), 93.

Element	Nature of Element
Fractal	The Relationship Between Small and Large
Adaptive	How We Change
Interdependent and Decentralized	Who We Are and How We Share
Nonlinear and Iterative	The Pace and Pathways of Change
Resilient, Rooted In Transformative Justice	How We Recover and Transform
Creating More Possibilities	How We Move Towards Life

In the study and practice of emergent strategy, there are core principles that have emerged and that guide us in learning and using this idea and method in the world. I gather them here with the expectation that they will grow.

- Small is good, small is all. (The large is a reflection of the small.)
- Change is constant. (Be like water.)[5]
- There is always enough time for the right work.
- There is a conversation in the room that only these people at this moment can have.[6] Find it.
- Never a failure, always a lesson.[7]
- Trust the People. (If you trust the people, they become trustworthy, and/or the necessary boundaries become clear.)[8]

---

5. "You must be shapeless, formless, like water. When you pour water in a cup, it becomes the cup. When you pour water in a bottle, it becomes the bottle. When you pour water in a teapot, it becomes the teapot. Water can drip and it can crash. Become like water my friend." Bruce Lee, *Bruce Lee: A Warrior's Journey* (Warner Home Video, 2000).
6. Idea articulated by Taj James in the co-facilitation of environmental justice resource redistribution initiative Building Equity and Alignment's inaugural meeting in 2013.
7. Rihanna has this concept tattooed on her chest.
8. This is an inversion of the quote "If you don't trust the people, they become un-

- Move at the speed of trust.[9] Focus on critical connections more than critical mass—build the resilience by building the relationships.
- Less prep, more presence.
- What you pay attention to grows.

And here are the elements of emergent strategy in more detail, and paired with their most relevant principles:

Fractal: The relationship between the small and the large. The large is made up of the smallest things, patterns repeat at scale. Help people see, celebrate, and build on the small shifts they are making.

Principle: Small is good, small is all, the large is a reflection of the small.

Intentional Adaptation: We are constantly changing—the more ease we bring to how we change, and the more intention we bring to our daily lives, the more that change can serve our vision. Help people change with intention. Not just react, not move into scarcity thinking where we have to handle every crisis, but adapt in ways that move us towards where we want to go.

Principle: Change is constant (be like water). Freeze bullshit, move like rapids when collective energy is flowing. As the facilitator, you need to continuously transform to meet and guide the room. Less prep, more presence.

Interdependent / Decentralized: Attend to the relationships and power dynamics in the rooms you hold, creating structures that support authentic, intimate relationships, mutual transformation, and collaboration.

Principles: There is always enough time for the right work. There's a conversation that only these people at this moment can

---

trustworthy," from Stephen Mitchell's translation, Lao Tzu, *Tao Te Ching* (New York: HarperCollins, 1988). I added the line about boundaries here because there are instances when trustworthiness would need more time than we can, or are willing, to give it.

9. This is communications strategist Mervyn Marcano's remix of Stephen Covey's "speed of trust" concept.

have. Help people see themselves. Help them harness the full potential of their work, intention, skill, and capacity in this moment.

Trust the people, they become trustworthy—or the necessary boundaries become clear. Sometimes group capacity, time, or other resources aren't aligned to support each person's arc towards trustworthiness. In those times, you need boundaries to keep the forward motion.

Nonlinear / Iterative: Change comes from cumulative shifts. Reflect to groups how they are accumulating change…or not. Reflect to groups what they are practicing—both in and out of alignment with their values.

Principles: Never a failure, always a lesson—help people find the lesson. What you pay attention to grows. Move at the speed of trust.

Transformative Justice / Resilience: Make room for the inevitable presence of socialized oppression. Keep a systemic view on it, even if it appears as individual behavior. Recover from oppression together by addressing it at the root. Seek understanding of what and who needs to be in the center of the struggle in the room, as all oppressions are usually present, but not equally weighted in each group.

Principle: Move at the speed of trust. Focus on critical connections more than critical mass. Build the resilience by building the relationships. We cannot build highly effective mass movements without trust at the core. Trust is slow until it is fast.

Creating More Possibilities: In healthy ecosystems there are many ways to be and many ways to grow, many paths to the future. Make room for us/the group to stay visionary. As facilitator, create the possibility of more time spent on our revolutionary goals.

Principles: Less prep, more presence. The less you pre-process, the more you are actually present, the more possibilities are available in the room.

What you pay attention to grows. Bring attention to the small, to each step people make towards each other, towards their work.

Make room for many possibilities, especially early in a process. Help groups learn to tolerate many paths in the pursuit of best options, versus reducing to less satisfying solutions in the rush to end the discomfort of the unknown. Bring attention to presence and the allotment of solutions. Change is constant.

*
**

Since *Emergent Strategy: Shaping Change, Changing Worlds* was published, I have identified some additional facilitation principles:

Begin by Listening. This core principle from Allied Media Projects is also a best practice for facilitation.[10] Ask questions, find out what people need, listen to what people say and don't say. Begin by listening to your own truths and feelings, and listening to each other.

Transform Yourself to Transform the World. This guidance, articulated by Grace Lee Boggs, is facilitation and mediation gold.[11] How you are, how you show up, invites a quality of presence from participants. If you want to change what *is* possible in the room, change what *you believe* is possible. Change how present you are, increase your rigor, focus your energy. Invite participants to have the same power to transform themselves to transform what is possible in the room, in the group.

What We Practice Is What We Are. What do we *say* we're practicing? What are we *actually* practicing? What do we *want* to be practicing? Practice is how we become what we long to be.

Name What Is, Make More Possible. We must deal in reality. It is nearly impossible for people to build trust over time if they cannot name and face what is actually happening. If we don't fully understand where we have come from, what created us, and where

---

10. See www.alliedmedia.org/networkprinciples.

11. Grace Lee Boggs is a Detroit ancestor and author of *Living for Change* and *The Next American Revolution*.

we are, then we are building our future on quicksand. By building a shared analysis of what's real, you create more possibilities for things the group can actually do.

Release Perfection, Relinquish Judgment. You are not necessarily right. And you are not better than any of these participants. They are living their lives and learning their lessons on behalf of the species, just like you. If you cannot support them without judgment and superiority, then you are not the right facilitator for them. "Perfection is a commitment to habitual self-doubt," teaches Prentis Hemphill. Create spaces that support participants to learn to trust themselves.

Create a Culture of Celebration—Pivot Towards Pleasure. It seems simple—but people stay more engaged in a space where they are enjoying each other, and feel celebrated and appreciated. Small, personal celebrations help fuel groups through the hard work, reminding them that they are humans together, regardless of the external pressures they face.

Invitation Goes Further Than Manipulation. It can be very tempting to use charm and pressure to bend a group to your will. Especially if you tell yourself that your will is just to help them achieve their goals. But if you manipulate them to completion, the results won't stick, because they didn't do the work to actually get to the conclusion themselves. Invite them, continuously, towards their own vision, into their own rigor. Invite them to participate in their own liberation.

Release *Your* Way to Feel *The* Way. If you are overly convinced that you know the right way, you will not be able to support the group to find the way of the collective. There are absolutely times when your perspective or opinion is the necessary ingredient for the collective to take a next step. With time you will learn the subtle art of when to speak up (rarely) and when to listen and support (mostly). Primarily, you listen and support and keep opening more room for the group.

Time Can Bend. It's so powerful to play with time. Cultures with long memories, still connected to their oldest ways, know that time is nonlinear, circular, mysterious. When we are facilitating a space and we remember that time can bend, we focus not on time scarcity but on the people in the room, the presence, and the work that must be done. I have been in so many rooms where we bent time, expanding it for a big emotion to move through, reversing it to undo a harm, finding ourselves satisfied well before our planned ending time. I always consider that maybe we didn't bend it, but the universe, a great spirit, approved of our work and opened for us.

Soundtrack While Writing this Book

My *Jazz Vocalist Women* playlist on Spotify (which has been with me at crucial moments for every book so far)

Love and Rage: Loving Our Anger playlist on Spotify

Celebrating One Step playlist on Spotify

Happiness Frequency videos on YouTube[12]

The *Crystal Singing Bowl* playlist by April Forest on Spotify

Black is King/The Gift, Beyoncé

Frank Ocean

Justin Bieber

Moses Sumney

Shantel May

serpentwithfeet, especially *Psychic*

Hamilton, sung by the original Broadway cast.

Lianne Le Havas, especially *Paper Thin, Weird Fishes* (actually I love the whole radio station playlist Spotify builds around *Weird Fishes*)

Megan Thee Stallion's album *Good News*

Taylor Swift's *Folklore* and *Evermore*

Beautiful Chorus

Beverly Glenn Copeland, especially *Let Us Dance*

---

12. My favorite is from Greenred Productions, called *Happiness Frequency: Serotonin, Dopamine, Endorphin Release Music, Binaural Beats Meditation.*

Assessments

In *Emergent Strategy* there's a set of assessments that I created myself. They do the job, but even as I was creating them, I was aware of my limitations: surely there was a better way to create tools that people can use to understand where they are related to a set of skills or conditions. I considered reaching out to my expert researcher friend Zuri Tai to help, but by the time I realized I wanted that, it was too late in the journey.

Fortunately, this time, Zuri was available when I remembered the assessments for this book, and my, my, my does she have a gift for community-based research. Zuri did a beautiful job translating my chaos of questions into a process that will help you assess your group's culture, functionality, emergent strategy capacity, purpose, and the presence of power dynamics.

There is also a facilitation self-assessment, a co-facilitation assessment, facilitation intake questions, and a mediation assessment.

Group Assessments

Group Efficiency Assessment (Check the statement in each row that applies best to your group)			
We are often able to set shared goals ___ (4)	Sometimes we are able to set shared goals ___ (3)	Rarely are we able to set shared goals ___ (2)	We have not tried to set shared goals ___ (1)
We are often comfortable sharing responsibility ___ (4)	Sometimes we are comfortable sharing responsibility ___ (3)	Rarely are we comfortable sharing responsibility ___ (2)	We have not tried to share responsibility ___ (1)
We are often able to meet shared goals ___ (4)	Sometimes we are able to meet shared goals ___ (3)	Rarely are we able to meet shared goals ___ (2)	We have not tried to meet shared goals ___ (1)
We are often creating impact beyond our group ___ (4)	Sometimes we are creating impact beyond our group ___ (3)	Rarely are we creating impact beyond our group ___ (2)	We have not tried to create impact beyond our group ___ (1)
Each answer in this column =4 *Total score ___*	*Each answer in this column=3* *Total score ___*	*Each answer in this column=2* *Total score ___*	*Each answer in this column=1* *Total score ___*
			Grand total (Add all scores) ___

Group Relationship Assessment (Check the statement in each row that applies best to your group)

We often feel **joyful** during and/or after meetings ___ (4)	Sometimes we feel **joyful** during and/or after meetings ___ (3)	We rarely feel **joyful** during and/or after meetings ___ (2)	We have not felt **joyful** during and/or after meetings ___ (1)	
We are often **vulnerable** with each other ___ (4)	Sometimes we are **vulnerable** with each other ___ (3)	Rarely are we **vulnerable** with each other ___ (2)	We have not tried to be **vulnerable** with each other ___ (1)	
We feel a strong **connection** to others in the group ___ (4)	We feel a growing **connection** to others in the group ___ (3)	We feel the possibility of **connection** to others in the group ___ (2)	We feel it's unlikely that we'll have **connection** in the group ___ (1)	
We often feel **enriched** during and/or after meetings ___ (4)	Sometimes we feel **enriched** during and/or after meetings ___ (3)	We rarely feel **enriched** during and/or after meetings ___ (2)	We have not felt **enriched** during and/or after meetings ___ (1)	
Each answer in this column =4	*Each answer in this column=3*	*Each answer in this column=2*	*Each answer in this column=1*	
Total score ___	*Total score* ___	*Total score* ___	*Total score* ___	**Grand total**
				(Add all scores) ___

Write the grand totals for the two assessments: ___ Efficiency ___ Relationship

A. high efficiency (score: 12–16), high relationship (score: 12–16)

- ○ These groups are exhibiting peak collective function, contributing to a clear mission and meeting goals. We can count on each other, trust each other, and enjoy each other.

B. low efficiency (score: 4–11), high relationship (score: 12–16)

- ○ These groups are survival bonded. We stay together, enjoy and maybe even love each other, but may not meet our stated goal or purpose.

C. high efficiency (score: 12–16), low relationship (score: 4–11)

- ○ These groups often form in response to a crisis. We get shit done but aren't sure we are all moving from the same intentions or if the outcomes are meaningful. The relationships feel temporary and people eventually get hurt.

D. low efficiency (score: 4–11), low relationship (score: 4–11)

- ○ Not accomplishing much for or beyond the group; gathering may be a coping mechanism because we don't want to be alone. Gathering is dysfunctional and lacks joy.

For high efficiency/high relationship read the Black Feminist Wisdom chapter

For low efficiency/high relationship scores read Creating More Possibilities, p. 178

For high efficiency/low relationship scores read Fractal Facilitation, p. 100

For low efficiency/low relationship scores read Interdependent/Decentralized Facilitation, p. 134

Group Function Assessment

1. How often do they need breaks?
    a) ____ Every 60-90 minutes, often after a piece of work is completed or reaches the satisfaction of a next step
    b) ____ Every 30-60 minutes, and conversation is easily moved into tangents
    c) ____ Never, or need to be reminded that breaks are an option
    d) ____ Right when the group is on the verge of taking action or landing a decision

2. What do they use their breaks for?
    a) ____ Bathroom, snacks, connecting to each other personally, deepening the work in the room
    b) ____ Talking to each other, doing work on other projects, second guessing the work that's moving in the room
    c) ____ Work. You have to remind them to use bathroom and go outside of the meeting space
    d) ____ Fomenting dissent or disillusionment

3. What is the tone in the room when disagreement arises?
    a) ____ Competent, turning towards it with solution mind
    b) ____ Fear of conflict, resistance to name what's going on
    c) ____ Unemotional, pushing for quick resolution that doesn't go to the root of the issue
    d) ____ Avoidance, checking out

4. How do they move through disagreements?
    a) ____ With integrity, attending to necessary root systems of the conflict but not wasting time
    b) ____ Struggle to stick to political lines, make arguments personal
    c) ____ Stick to the surface issues, rush to move things along in ways that leave issues to fester
    d) ____ Struggling to speak the truth in the room, lots of side conversations

5. Are they dysfunctionally high in session? Or show up late after nights of partying?
   a) ____ Rarely, and/or collectively after big moments of work
   b) ____ Often, struggling to be present for the work
   c) ____ No, and they judge each other for any signs of fun or coping
   d) ____ They aren't present enough to tell what is causing the low participation

6. Do they follow through on tasks and commitments?
   a) ____ Yes, they are accountable to each other
   b) ____ No, but they talk about the reasons why
   c) ____ Yes, but with conflict in how the tasks are done, working competitively instead of collaboratively
   d) ____ No, tasks seem to disappear into a black hole

7. Are the power dynamics clear in the room? (Who has power? How did they get it?)
   a) ____ Yes. The power dynamics are clear and the group is comfortable with them.
   d) ____ Not quite—there's a story that power is fully shared.
   c) ____ Yes, but people don't think it's necessarily fair, or know how to change it.
   d) ____ No, and the power that is in the room is used to delay action rather than move it.

Count the number of a's_____ ; of b's_____ ; of c's_____; of d's_____

If you selected mostly a's then you're working with an engaged group. They use emergent practices, are usually present, in high relationship with each other and have a clear understanding of power and boundaries.

If you selected mostly b's then you're working with a resistant group. They are often second-guessing the work and prone to conflict or getting stuck and distracted. They are in low relationship with each other. They may have high energy but low focus, and are unclear on the power relations and boundaries in the group.

If you selected mostly c's then you're working in a driven group. They are task oriented and likely have short-term high focus. They are usually in low relationship, yet may be able to move work forward. However they lack emergent practices and clear understanding of how to negotiate power and boundaries.

If you selected mostly d's then you're working in an avoidant group. They are more likely to spend energy debating or ruminating about what should be done than actually doing any work. They are usually in low relationship with each other and lack an understanding of how power is playing out in the group. Boundaries are often ignored.

Quick assessment to gauge Emergent Strategy in the room:		
Are they practicing authenticity? Are people sharing real needs and making real offers? Are they comfortable with vulnerability?	**a. Yes, most of the time** **b. No, not really**	If no, go to Boundaries Can Be Love By Prentis Hemphill & Chapter Seven Transformative Justice/Resilience Facilitation
Is interdependence evident among the group? Are people striving to be in right-relationship with each other? What is the smallest unit in the room? Are people resisting the tendency to act as individuals?	**a. Yes, most of the time** **b. No, not really**	If no, go to Chapter Six: Interdependent/ Decentralized Facilitation
Are they available and present? Are they showing up on time? Are they engaged in discussion? Are they minimizing distractions?	**a. Yes, most of the time** **b. No, not really**	If no, go to Stay Black and Breathe By Alexis Pauline Gumbs & "Problem" Participants and What They Need
Are healthy patterns emerging? Is the group honoring shared agreements? Are patterns such as intimacy over isolation; collaboration over critique, and flexibility over rigidity present?	**a. Yes, most of the time** **b. No, not really**	If no, go to An Invitation to Brave Space By Micky ScottBey Jones & Practices: Increasing Access in the Room & "Problem" Participants and What They Need
Are they adapting? Are they comfortable changing when conditions change? Are they moving in organic ways?	**a. Yes, most of the time** **b. No, not really**	If no, go to Chapter Four: Intentional Adaptation Facilitation
Are they practicing justice with one another? Are they committed to resolving small and large conflicts? Are they practicing accountability?	**a. Yes, most of the time** **b. No, not really**	If no, go to Chapter Seven Transformative Justice/Resilience Facilitation
Are they creating and holding boundaries? Are they maintaining confidentiality? Are they holding boundaries around sexual relationships?	**a. Yes, most of the time** **b. No, not really**	If no, go to An Invitation to Brave Space By Micky ScottBey Jones & Boundaries Can Be Love By Prentis Hemphill

Additional Group Assessments

Assessing the Container aka Group Purpose: What brought you together?		
1. Are you gathering in response to an event with heightened sense of urgency? **(Reactive orientation)**	**If yes, start with:** Chapter 8: Creating More Possibilities Facilitation	**Emergent Strategy Principles:** -Trust the people, they become trustworthy or the necessary boundaries become clear. - Move at the speed of trust. **Emergent Strategy Elements:** -Creating more possibilities -Resilience & Transformative Justice -Interdependence / Decentralization:
2. Are you gathering in response to a shared need or agreed upon desire to transform? **(Proactive orientation)**	**If yes, start with:** Chapter 5 Nonlinear/Iterative Facilitation & Chapter 4 Intentional Adaptation Facilitation	**Emergent Strategy Principles:** -There is always enough time for the right work. -There is a conversation that only these people at this moment can have. -Change is constant -Small is good, small is all **Emergent Strategy Elements:** -Intentional Adaptation -Non-linear and iterative -Interdependence /Decentralization
3. Are you gathering specifically for emotional or spiritual support, with a focus on healing? **(Nurture & Nest** The group has shared trauma history and goals.)	**If yes, start with:** The consequences of denying grief & Chapter 3: Fractal Facilitation	**Emergent Strategy Principles:** -Less prep, more presence. -What you pay attention to grows **Emergent Strategy Elements:** -Fractal -Non-linear and Iterativeimpact
4. Are you gathering to learn or gain new skills or practices, with a focus on mastery? **(Train and Prepare** The group has shared goals.)	**If yes, start with:** Chapter 5 Nonlinear/Iterative Facilitation	**Emergent Strategy Principles:** -Small is good, small is all -Never a failure, always a lesson -What you pay attention to grows **Emergent Strategy Elements:** -Fractal
5. Are you gathering to develop a network for community support and connection? **(Building community** The group has shared traits and values.)	**If yes, read:** Chapter 6: Interdependent/ Decentralized Facilitation	**Emergent Strategy Principles:** - There is a conversation in the room that only these people at this moment can have. -Trust the people - Move at the speed of trust **Emergent Strategy Elements:** -Interdependence /Decentralization
6. Are you gathering to recover from conflict or shared trauma? **(Restoring relationships** The group has shared goals)	**If yes, read:** Chapter 7 Transformative Justice / Resilience Facilitation	**Emergent Strategy Principles:** -Trust the people - Move at the speed of trust **Emergent Strategy Elements:** -Resilience & Transformative Justice

What are the existing power dynamics?	
1. Do participants work at the same organization?	Yes/No
2. Do participants work for or supervise someone in the group?	Yes/No
3. Do participants have a romantic history with someone in the group?	Yes/No
4. Do participants have shared trauma or history of harm with someone in the group?	Yes/No
5. Do most of the participants know each other?	Yes/No

If you answered yes to any of these questions, then take time to consider the power relations that people are engaging in that pre-date the group and are outside of your control.

Read the "What Is Principled Struggle?" section of the next chapter.

Facilitator Assessments

Elements in Facilitation Self-Assessment/Journaling:

The Self-Assessment is a tool to deepen your understanding of your facilitation approach. These questions can be used in a journaling practice or before you do the following co-facilitation assessment. It will be helpful to revisit these questions and your answers on a regular basis.

- How do I orient to small changes and successes?
- How have I adapted to change in my own life?
- Am I comfortable trusting someone else to hold space with me? Why or why not?
- Am I comfortable facilitating groups when the conditions change? Why or why not?
- What are the main practices I bring to my facilitation?
- How do I orient to shared power? (What feedback have those I've shared power with given me?)
- What resilience practices am I in?
- How do I bring my focus to solutions?
- In what ways am I right for this group? Do I share identity, experience, culture, capacity, and/or economics?
- In what ways am I wrong for this group? Do I have dissimilar identity, experience, culture, capacity, and/or economics?

Co-Facilitation Assessment Questions (For A Conversation With A Potential Co-Facilitator):

The Co-Facilitation Assessment is a tool to deepen understanding and maintain communication between facilitators. These questions can be asked at the beginning of the relationship and revisited regularly.

This assessment will help you understand how to communicate well with each other; how you approach facilitation; how you handle conflict; and how you manage clients.

- Your facilitation approach
  - How do you understand the work of facilitation?
  - How do you usually show up in your facilitation role?
  - What is your capacity to facilitate in this season? (Are you busy? Balancing a lot?)
  - What helps you show up as your best in a facilitation partnership?
  - What hinders you from showing up as your best in a facilitation partnership?
  - How would you handle it if I did something you didn't agree with during our facilitation?
  - If there is a breakdown how do you respond, cope, and provide support?
- Communication
  - How will I know when you are not pleased?
  - How will I know when you are satisfied?
  - How do you know when you're overwhelmed? How might you communicate that to me?
  - What happens when your capacity shifts (grows or lessens)? How might you communicate that to me?
- Organization & Practices
  - What is your process for understanding the facilitation landscape with a new client?
  - How do you build your agendas?
  - How do you handle booking, scheduling, billing, late payments, etc.?
- History
  - Have you been in a co-facilitation relationship before?
  - What did you like about it? What didn't you like about it?
  - Have you worked with this client, or any of the individuals in this group, before?

Assessment Questions for Potential Facilitation Clients

- Why? Questions

- ○ Why this? Why are we having this meeting/gathering/conversation?
- ○ Why now? Why is this conversation needed now?
- ○ Why us? Why are we the right people to call in this gathering?
- ○ Why does it matter? Why is this relevant?
- Who? Questions
  - ○ Who are we accountable to?
  - ○ Who grows us?
  - ○ Who is actually down to do the work?
  - ○ Who has the skills we need?
- How? Questions
  - ○ How will we be in this process?
  - ○ How will this have impact?
  - ○ How can we embody our values?
- When? Questions
  - ○ When is this work needed by?
  - ○ When can we start?
  - ○ When will we be finished?
- What? Questions
  - ○ What can we do together?
  - ○ What excites and enlivens us?
  - ○ What will serve our people?
  - ○ What is at the root of our work?

Mediation Assessment

Mediation is the right move if:	Mediation is the wrong move if:
___ Both/all parties are open to mediation	___ All parties are not ready to discuss and/or acknowledge their role in the conflict
___ There is no threat of physical danger if the two parties are in the same space	___ Emotions are still running high and the likelihood of respectful dialogue is low
___ There is a pattern of misunderstanding, hurt feelings, or unjust power dynamics that needs adjusting, or a boundary that needs to be set	___ There is a threat of physical danger if the two parties are in the same space
___ There is a clearly satisfiable outcome (such as an apology, a boundary, or a clarification)	___ The parties do not believe resolution is possible or if they can't imagine a satisfiable outcome (such as an apology, a boundary, or a clarification)
___ The parties are open to being accountable and honest	

Black Feminist Wisdom

As I was crafting this book, I thought about my lineage as a facilitator—the way I walk with whispers of Harriet Tubman, Fanny Lou Hamer, Ella Baker in my spine, how I feel guided and driven forward by their bold legacies.[1]

Then I got excited as I thought about the living Black feminists I have gotten to work alongside of and learn from in this lifetime. I am of a lineage of women who have held space and been unseen, intentionally and unintentionally, contributing to movement from the root system of rooms where movement happens. We are satisfied when we see the collective advance, we are satisfied when we see the group grow towards each other, when we help them galvanize their power and leave a mark on history. It's a role that isn't always uplifted, especially while we live. But I'm also of a generation of Black women risking the dangers of demanding a space in the stories that get told, women who are whispering and then yelling, "I dug a trench on this battleground too, the day we win, my blood will be in that soil too." A generation of women who step forward with the truth of heartfelt contribution and get pushed and pulled back, told in myriad ways to stay in our place, fulfill the simple prescribed roles that can only benefit patriarchy, white supremacy, and capitalism. What I've noticed in this generation

---

1. Who is in your facilitation lineage? Draw it out, write it up, add their names to your altars, donate to their legacies!

is a willingness to take responsibility for what we know and what we need to learn. But still, so many of the fingerprints on the clay of this historic moment are unknown, under-recognized, too easily dismissed, their contributions an invisible vase when movement gets and gives their flowers.

I'm in a rich garden because of the lineage and these comrades. I could, and may, fill a book with only these voices one day, there are so many wisdoms to share.

I reached out to a handful of them—"please give me a few words of your facilitation wisdom." I am astounded by what they responded with. Here is a bit about these facilitator-contributors I have been honored to be yoked up with over the years:

Alexis Pauline Gumbs is a magical fairy teacher—a writer, facilitator, and doula who has been teaching me to breathe since we first met. Several times I have been in a room and looked over and noticed that a beam of light had found her, particularly. And that she was smiling, leaning in, and her eyebrows were up with curiosity, or wonder. You can feel the impact of breath in her system.

Autumn Brown is a quintuple Sag mother of three living children who facilitates with a sword in each hand, laughing, smoke rising from her skirts. She thinks like a poet economist, moves like a diva, and holds space like a theologian. Autumn was the first person to show me how consensus could be done with efficiency, while still deepening relationships. She has shaped a lot of our current movement success, but keeps it quiet, behind the scenes, part of a collective effort. She is my sister, and I look up to her.

Prentis Hemphill is a spark-of-god type negro. When Prentis brings their attention to your trouble, your wound, your need, they help you rediscover the simplicity of miracle, the miracle of agency, the agency available in each and every day. Prentis has taught me a masters class in boundaries-as-liberation—they let me understand that they love me and I can love them, with boundaries.

Sage Crump is a quiet storm goddess with a rolling thunder laugh. Sage invites me into rooms where I get to belong, and to sing. Sage has waved off affirmation in ways that never feel like false humility, that always feel like, "Yes, all is love, let's get on with it." She embodies emergent strategy, and she understands the subtle, complex work we are doing to get free in our daily con-struction of life. Here, she makes a case for every instance of facili-tation as a practice ground for the future.

Makani Themba is a hearth keeper, an altar builder, and she did not come to play. She loves liberation movements hard, and can correct the course of a conversation with a withering look. She is concerned with Black power, Black creativity, and Black joy. Every time we speak she is on her way to hear Black music. I love when we get to co-facilitate because our approaches are vastly different, and the groups that call on us need the combination of us, the balance of us. She pushes me to say what I know in the room, she calls us all in as co-strategists of future movement.

N'Tanya Lee is more a teacher than a facilitator, as she will tell you herself. Being in a room with her is to be dazzled by her standards, her intellect, and her smile. She introduced an accessible framework for principled struggle at a key moment in the modern movement for Black liberation—I have zero doubt that part of our current momentum is rooted in this gift she gave us.

Malkia Devich Cyril is a warrior of love. As the founder of the Center for Media Justice, Malkia has done incomparable work to ensure that we maintain control over our voice, our Internet access, our movement communication tools. She has also experienced a massive amount of intimate loss, and teaches us every day how to continue moving towards justice with a grieving heart. I feel that grief, constant, compiling, unspoken, and sloppily held, is at the root of much of our movement dysfunction. Malkia shows us what we need to face.

Micky ScottBey Jones is a southern organizer poet who wrote a piece called *An Invitation to Brave Space* that assuaged something within me that always cringed when participants would demand a safe space. I wanted a model that allowed me to be honest about what is possible. Micky felt for it, wrote it, and gave us permission to include it in these pages.

Adaku Utah is the kind of incredible Black unicorn who would partner with Harriet Tubman to create an Apothecary, a healing space, an experiment in abundant horizontal care. Harri-et's Apothecary is only one of the ways Adaku leads and serves movement—she is also giving us reproductive justice futures at the National Network of Abortion Funds. Her model for care bear teams (in the "Interdependent/Decentralized Facilitation" chapter) will help us all structurally increase the love and care in our movement spaces.

Ejeris Dixon is a formidable strategist with a killer grin and easy command of any room she chooses to lead. Co-editor of *Beyond Survival*, Ejeris has a lot to teach us about how we practice transformative justice and community safety. For this text, she guides us in the work of facilitating spaces that are safer, where we as facilitators are accountable to those we hold.

Paris Hatcher is an old school, whiskey-dipped Black feminist who has been transforming the landscape of reproductive justice, and in the past few years tying Black feminist futures to our facilitation skills. For this text she reflects on why and how she's been creating a training path for facilitation.

Inca Mohamed is the facilitator I want to be when I grow up—kind, funny, involved, boundaried, fascinated by life, relatable, glamorous, and curious. In this book, Inca shares with us what it looks like to facilitate for the long haul, to continue to be a necessary offer to movement as times, conditions, and practices evolve.

*
**

Stay Black And Breathe

by Alexis Pauline Gumbs

Facilitation is a Black art.

Why?

Because every facilitation process is a journey into the unknown. A possible future. A bright Black field of possibility. That's why we need facilitators as guides. Because it is not easy to face the death of how things have been and to open up to the vulnerability of how things could be. But we must.

Every facilitator is a doula, easing some necessary rebirth organizational, political, interpersonal, or otherwise for some folks who want change. The future is Black because we don't know it yet. And that's the beautiful thing. But if you haven't noticed, folks are scared to death of Black beauty. Even Black folks are socialized to fear the Blackness of the universe, the future, ourselves. A Black sky of infinite stars is terrifying to any of us living, organizing, and relating to each other in a white supremacist colonized frame that has trained us to pretend we already know. To pretend that what matters to us most is under our control.

It isn't.

Are you breathing?

Consider the top two things people say they are afraid of:

1. Speaking in public
2. Death

Every facilitation experience confronts both. And when people are afraid, they do not breathe.

I assert that your primary responsibility as a facilitator is to keep people breathing in the face of their greatest fears—including rejection, not knowing, being wrong, losing something, and the future. And you do it for the sake of what the people you collaborate with want most: change, possibility, connection, revelation, clarity, purpose, futures.

So here are some things I have learned about breathing as a facilitation practice:

Breathing Has a (Black Feminist) History.

Seven years ago I crafted a breathing practice for myself based on the words of Black feminist ancestors. My goal was to rededicate my breathing to those revolutionary ancestors who have made my life possible. (Essex Hemphill said, "I love myself enough to be who I am.") I needed a chanting practice suffused with the wisdom of the people who are the source of the freedom and peace I experience in this lifetime. (Audre Lorde said, "I am who I am doing what I came to do.") My practice was to chant these quotations 108 times as the center of my daily meditation practice.

After practicing for a year, I shared the first twenty-one of these meditations with my community through the Black Feminist Breathing Chorus on blackfeministbreathing.tumblr.com (June Jordan said, "We are the ones we've been waiting for."), a Black Feminist Breathing Tour of the United States, and a Black Feminist Breathing Retreat in Magnolia, Mississippi, on the fiftieth anniversary of the Mississippi Freedom Summer (Fannie Lou Hamer said, "Nobody's Free Until Everybody's Free.").

Black feminist performance artists like Laurie Carlos have used intentional breath as a portal-making practice intentionally for decades. Carlos's close collaborator and friend Ntozake Shange drew on what Franz Fanon called "combat breathing" as a poetic practice to respond to violence against Black women. My breathing exists in this legacy and others.

What is the legacy of your breathing?

You Breathe First

Remember what they told you on the airplane? Make sure you are breathing before you try to put a breathing mask on anyone else. What is your relationship to breathing? Study it. When does your breath deepen, quicken, shallow, catch? Learning this about yourself will support you to be intentional about your own breath and present to the messages in the breathing of people around you. As you prepare to facilitate, be sure to incorporate grounding practices for yourself (meditation, physical practice, connection to loved ones) that allow to you breathe as freely as you can.

Facilitation Is Breathing in Public

When my sister Kyla was giving birth to her first child, I was her doula. It was my first time being anyone's doula and my first time being present for a birth. Afterwards, Kyla's gratitude feedback was that my breathing reminded her to breathe. As you facilitate, you are modeling one way it looks to be present to birth, change, and possibility. Your breathing itself is guide and evidence for everyone with you that we can breathe through change.

Breathing Is a Shared Resource

As a facilitator there are a number of ways to make the movement of invisible air a visible practice. Taking breaths together towards the beginning of a session, asking for a deep breath after or during a transitional moment, and asking folks to study and learn from their own breathing during your time together are just a few of the infinite ways you can make breathing a shared and tangible resource for the process.

The Air We Breathe Is Dedicated Air

Yes. Breathing is shared. The air in the room in necessary to everyone and impacts everyone involved. I think of every facilitation space as a spiritual ecosystem of dedicated air. I often ask folks to verbally dedicate their participation to someone who is not in the room with us, but who is part of the reason that the participant brought their breathing body into the room. The varied breathing of the people of the room is also a field through which folks who are no longer breathing, our ancestors, can travel into the room. Our breathing also carries memories and intentions for living people who are not in the room.

Breathing Is Particular

And we all breathe differently. Our relationships to breath are impacted by our different bodies, our breathing practices, our relationships to the people in the room and the institutions we are engaging and myriad other factors. The pace, the character, and the messages in the breath of each person are crucial. Our breathing can be as unifying and as particular as it needs to be.

Physiologists have proven that when people constrict their breathing out of fear they lower the amount of oxygen going to their brain. I also believe that when I cut off my breathing I am limiting the space ancestors have to connect with me and guide me through the moment. Millions of us are holding our breath and hoping a change comes worthy of our exhalations. What I know is that if we breathe for a change we will have more access to each other and the energies that can move us through this moment and the next.

Breathing is Sacred

Our breathing is precious because it is contingent and particular and should never be taken for granted. How miraculous is it that we are together across the planet interchanging molecules held by the same sky? The pandemic we've experienced has changed our relationships to breathing and facilitation. It also means facilitation and breathing work continues to happen, even if not between people in the same rooms sharing the same air molecules. As we all continue to learn how to be more intentional about how our breathing impacts each other's well-being, I am in awe of how our breathing continues to connect us across space and time. Breathing together over video-conference technology and through pre-recorded content is still breathing together. The energetic impact we have on each other is important for how we feel, move, and make decisions in the moment. And it is also a reminder of the larger truth: our energy is not limited by space or time, it persists. Even across death. Our breathing is sacred because the energy that connects us is older than any of the structures we are unlearning and will persist beyond the imagination of this species. The energy moving through us, as air and so much more, is eternal. I call it love. Thank you for the love moving through you. With every breath.

*
* *

Consensus Reflection

by Autumn Brown

Back in the day when I led consensus trainings regularly, I would have groups do an activity called "Too Many Cooks." The design: each group receives a list of ingredients and has the same amount of time to design a meal, by consensus. The same list of ingredients would invariably produce wildly different meal proposals, a cornucopia of concepts that would make the judges of the Food Network's *Chopped* proud.

The goal and lesson of this activity was two-fold:

1) to give participants a low-stakes opportunity to try out the principles of consensus they had just learned (the catch—food is never actually a low stakes conversation—an early assumption that was rapidly dismantled by experience, which brings me to lesson two);

2) to help participants experience in real time the primary reasons groups who attempt to use consensus and fail, do so: unstated assumptions and unacknowledged differences in worldview. Whereas the dominant ideology of group process would have us assume that fissures arise in groups primarily from differences in opinion, or the process taking too long, or people not knowing how to be in conflict, the real problem is so much simpler and also so much harder to see: we think we agree because we think we mean the same things with our words, but we don't. The fissure is there long before the conflict arises.

And so, the recipe for making consensus work is simple, but the work is fierce. Ingredients include:

- Alignment
- Time (or timelessness, a spiritual practice of forgetting urgency)
- Trust (remembering each other)
- Principled Stance

When we need to reach consensus, we mix the following ingredients, and the resulting dish is quite magical.

Seek Alignment:

Are we the people who need to make this decision? If not, stop and gather. There are others who must be present in order for us to be in principled stance with and toward one another.

Create Time:

This may require us to use magic and bend time. Or it may be as simple as looking at scale and scope: what scope of decision can we make in the time we have? If we cannot figure out everything, then what is the plan for figuring out the other parts at a different time? We have to assess—is it important, urgent, and/or both? Give the time and space required of the subject. No shortcuts.

Extend Trust:

Someone once said, trust the people and they become trustworthy. This looks like allowing people their full humanity and their gifts. Are there folks who have greater knowledge and expertise? Give them room to be persuasive. Are there those who listen better than speak? Invite them to support synthesizing all of the best ideas into something greater. Is there a naysayer? Invite their critique as a part of the structure of making decisions.

Be in Principled Stance:

Know that you cannot meaningfully agree until you have meaningfully disagreed, and that disagreement requires honest assessment of ourselves and our conditions. Principled stance with and towards one another requires us to have an honest assessment, to disagree and then find alignment from *that* place. Then we know we can agree, and that it means something.

Seasoning is laughter and implementation. Don't forget that consensus is magic, and it heals us. When we fully consent, we are in our agency. In our agency we can do anything.

Boundaries Can Be Love

by Prentis Hemphill

I learned first about walls. I was raised by a great storm of a father and a mother who was kind, and sometimes fearful too. Our house could fill with yells and teeth-grinding fear almost as easily as it could fill with belly laughs and dancing. It was unpredictable, and almost worse than the rage was the uncertainty of where the next eruption would come from. So, I built walls as a child. Very literally forts, stiff couch-cushion blockades. My mother would say that I built forts just to sit in there and sweat, but I built them, actually, so I could breathe. I created a predictable space that could hold and protect me.

It wasn't until my twenties that I realized that I had become trapped in those walls. That my body had, along the way, calculated the risk of connection to be too high to engage. And from where I sat, the real me, in the seat of myself, I found it dangerous to reveal. I had forgotten how to get out of myself and really be with others.

Walls can seem a lot like boundaries, they're easy to confuse. But walls more likely become a rule. They erect themselves along a certainty, i.e. intimacy is unsafe or I'm too much to be in relationship with. They reinforce or create a static worldview that is transferable to other conditions, other relationships. They have a way of keeping you captive when they were once designed to keep you safe.

Boundaries, on the other hand, are responsive, movable, and highly dependent on real-time assessments. Boundaries are how you guide and protect your life energy. The skillful use of boundaries allow us to create proximity, intimacy, distance.

In 2006, I stopped talking to my father. The details aren't as important as the fact that I was fed up with cycles of rage and a struggle, fundamentally, to be considered. This wasn't the first time I'd gone periods without speaking to him, but this was different. I wasn't punishing him this time by retracting myself. I was creating space from a place of accepting that he wasn't, at least in that moment, going to shift—and without a shift I couldn't continue to engage. And for the first time, instead of maintaining reactivity to him, I settled. I focused instead on what need I longed for him to be able to fulfill, and strategized on how to otherwise get that need met. I wrote a letter saying as much to him, mailed it, and at the mailbox released expectations that anything at all would change.

In that decade of distance, I was fully resigned to never talk to him again. But the focus wasn't on talking to him or not talking to him as much as it was about recognizing that, behind whatever walls I might build, I longed for consistency in care, longed to be worth the risk of another's accountability. And instead of trying to force that in my parental relationship, I could seek it in my adult relationships, consciously and consensually.

In that, boundaries showed up one day as a revelation. A knowledge that emerged out of my own love practice with myself. Centered on the satisfaction of my own needs and yearnings, they clarified my relationships for me. I was carting my unconscious needs around less, looking to recreate my disappointment less. I was more often assessing the likelihood of satisfaction and creating opportunities for my needs to be met. I was trusting my assessments, disengaging earlier, when it became clear that I was only irritating my wound. And I learned, maybe most importantly, that there are degrees to engagement. I can titrate my vulnerability, my trust, the depth of connection without being inauthentic. Each relationship has its own unique recipe.

I celebrated my boundaries as a return of agency to my body. A practice of being present and honest.

Two years ago I called my father on a whim. I didn't plan it out, just picked up the phone because I was curious how he was. We talked for ten minutes, we gave the surface updates and hung up. Since then I've visited him maybe three times, all short porch visits—listening to my limits and honoring them. Last May, I was in my hometown for a morning and asked my father out to breakfast. Our longest visit to date. Over these years I've lost my reactivity to him. I think it's because I've also lost the need for him to change. I don't think this is for everyone and it is definitely not a stand-in for accountability. The lesson on boundaries was learned both in the distance and in the contact. We don't have to ever change the terms. But I did, and that speaks to another possibility of boundaries. They can change.

I wrote a note on social media about our relationship and on forgiveness—which is still something I'm learning so much about. I also wrote on boundaries, defining them as "the distance at which I could love me and you simultaneously." A friend took that last line and meme'd it and, over the next week, I got to see just how much the definition resonated with people. I think we struggle with boundaries because we forget their purpose. They don't hold up when they are not coupled with the work of loving ourselves. We might succumb instead to love habits that keep us unsatisfied and grasping, or we might close off to connection altogether. Boundaries, then, cannot be a passive practice. Boundaries give us the space to do the work of loving ourselves. They might be, actually, the first and fundamental expression of self-love. They also give us the space to love and witness others as they are, even those that have hurt us.

*
**

Facilitation as Experiments in Culture Creation

by Sage Crump

> "Cultural Apartheid and/or Cultural Integration is at the heart
> of all government (governance) and informs the way gover-
> nance … compels the exodus of people voluntarily or driven
> and raises complex questions of dispossession and recovery."
> —Toni Morrison, from *The Source of Self-Regard*

At its core, I like to describe facilitation as supporting a body of
people moving through a process. I keep my definition basic because there are so many ways facilitation can look. There are many
brilliant facilitators and each has a unique approach. A strong facilitator supports groups in shaping the experience they want to
have together. By moving through simple tasks, bodies of people,
from 10 to 10,000, set the parameters of how they want to be together and will always be the decision makers on where they land
at the end of the day, consciously or unconsciously.

I know some people think that it is the role of the facilitators
to "get them there." Get the people to do the things that they have
said they would do. Follow the agenda. Put away your phones. Be
present. All of these seem reasonable requests. Yet, I am reminded
of the writing of Antonio Gramsci and how common sense is a
tool of the dominant hegemonic culture, which, in this day, is the

culture of white supremacy. I have often been placed, portrayed, and readily accepted the role of facilitator as authoritarian in the room—the person whose job it is to wrangle the people and keep them on task. Lately I've also started to think about how I came to be in the rooms in the first place. It often looked like, a) some small group deciding on a body of work, b) calling/contacting me to build a way toward an end result, c) me showing up to a room and managing the time, personal dynamics, and all the contextual matters that impact the group's ability to make the end goal. This sounded reasonable to me for many years. But the more I started thinking deeply about the ways culture is made and how it is re-enforced, the more uncomfortable I became with how I was practicing as a facilitator. After twenty years of facilitating so many different kinds of spaces and groups, I found myself asking the questions: What exactly are we practicing through this model? What culture do I want to participate in? And how can the work I am doing in this moment support the transformation of the world we live in?

The works of Tema Okun, Linda Tuhiwai Smith, Intelligent Mischief, Cathy Cohen, Audre Lorde, Ishmael Reed, and Octavia Butler, as well as discussions about how culture is created and can shift with brilliant friends like Malkia Cyril, Tufara Waller Muhammed, kai lumumba barrow, Ashley Sparks, and muthi reed continue to help me ground a facilitation practice in the values I believe are important for transforming the world we currently live in into a culture that can hold self-determination, collective dignity, communal responsibility, and individual accountability. We are living culture in a way where we are not only making "products" together but making meaning of our values and work.

This reframe resembles a phenomenon of quantum physics called "superposition." The shortest definition of superposition is... things that can do opposite things at the same time. I turn to quantum physics because its core helps us hold complexity. I believe our ability to recognize, accept, and move with complexity is integral to how we dismantle the current state and build new ways of being with each other. The ability to engage complexity is directly tied to our ability to imagine. Facilitation as a practice rooted in culture building and superposition can help us integrate a complex understanding of the world.

All of these thoughts have led me to question what would happen if I approached every room I facilitated as an opportunity to support the creation of a culture of liberation, creativity, and inquiry. Culture is not accidental. Culture is a creation that can be tended to and focused in specific ways. Every time people are gathered together, the hegemony of dominant culture is playing out unless there is an intention to be/do otherwise. There are skills and capacities we need to live into the future we believe in and we can develop and practice them in the rooms that we facilitate.

Facilitation methods are ways we grow our emotional intelligence, collective decision making, alternative governance structures, and practice ways of connecting to the inherent dignity and humanity of each other. Through facilitation, we have the ability to elevate, amplify, and address the most deeply buried and least visible aspects of culture, aspects that feel like common sense but may not be what we need. Through facilitation, we make the time to engage one another in growing our understanding and practices around assumed and imagined political views, learning styles, gender roles, the value of time, and other definitions.

When we center the voices/visions of people othered by racialized capitalism, we are engaging the development of a deeper political understanding, and we are also shaping a culture at its heart, reckoning with historical injustices in our very bodies. With this mind on facilitation, we learn how to navigate discomfort together. A facilitator's role is not to make everyone comfortable. Our job is to help people through their discomfort while using all of the knowledge and feelings in the room to make meaning and take actions informed by the learning. Facilitated environments working in this way open up a space where people get to live into new roles/ new shapes. This includes the facilitator who can miss moments of human connection when, as I wrote earlier, traditional expectations of facilitation that typically involve a predominant energetic focus on a final product.

How many times has getting to the end of the agenda felt like the most important milestone?

As facilitators we are paid to meet our clients' needs and that can sometimes drive our motives. That is a very real and important factor. We all want to keep working at this thing we love to do. Being intentional about creating culture while facilitating it requires us as facilitators to find the brave spaces we are often asking participants to find. A facilitator's brave space is especially needed when we are facilitating justice-driven work. When we are facilitating to the agenda and not facilitating to the room of people in front of us and the current moment we are all experiencing, we miss the chance to reframe the collective's relative relationship to time and investment in each person's present humanity. That doesn't mean we don't keep the work moving forward. It does mean that how the work moves is shapeshifting in real time. The white supremacist heteropatriarchy culture's relationship to time makes us feel like there is never enough of it—that efficiency is of paramount importance. In a facilitated environment, we can decide not to be controlled by this way of keeping time, and yet be considerate of it.

As a facilitator you sometimes realize that there may be more to a conversation than the time allotted allows. You have decisions to make about what you are going to offer the group as a way forward. Here is the moment when you can invite everyone into trying something new. Something new can involve asking the group how they would like to proceed, offering suggestions that adjust the end goals of the day, and helping participants to breathe through the change. I know it may seem antithetical to the ways we understand the role of the facilitator to say that it doesn't matter if you get to the final product, but what you are doing is supporting everyone in the room to rethink prescriptions of time and productivity by placing importance on other happenings in the room, using time as simply a resource. We can both practice a culture in which time is abundant and we can turn success into a spectrum, a process that amplifies the value of every moment and increases our creativity and imagination as we work at finding a new way forward.

For emergent strategy, this is culture-building, culture-shifting. Success in a process is not about finding the one, big, perfect solution. **Emergent strategy is amplifying the importance of the incremental to impact the monumental.** Our facilitation spaces are locations of practice for learning and strengthening culture. Facilitators have tools to invite all the participants into a process, and one of our most overlooked methodologies is the making of community agreements. Community agreements are the first moments in a gathering where you invite folks into a collective practice of culture building. Here you build consent for a collective endeavor, and consent is integral to any experiment. Community agreements provide an opening for a conversation about culture and a written document of the collective vision of the practice you all will be in together.

I was recently in a group being facilitated by a well-known and well-paid consulting firm. The facilitator opened with Ground Rules. Right out of the gate, I had an inkling about the nature of the facilitation style and the role we as participants were expected to play. We were expected to be quiet and follow the rules set by facilitators. We were never asked for consent on how to proceed or about our capacity to engage in the different discussions during the day or whether it would be better for us if we moved agenda items around. It felt pretty clear to me that these facilitators had accepted the white supremacist heteropatriarchal capitalist culture of authoritarianism as one of their core values, a common "best practice." These are not practices that build a culture of care and collaboration. We can use simple tools like community agreements to reframe power and authority with collective care, agency, and support.

We can do better. We can source these intimate moments of learning together to shift the foundations of society. If cultural change does precede political change, then practicing, learning, and consciously iterating towards a culture we believe can hold the highest vision for the world we are making is paramount. When we open ourselves to this calling as facilitators, facilitation spaces provide the opportunity and all of the needed ingredients to build pathways for the emergence of a new culture.

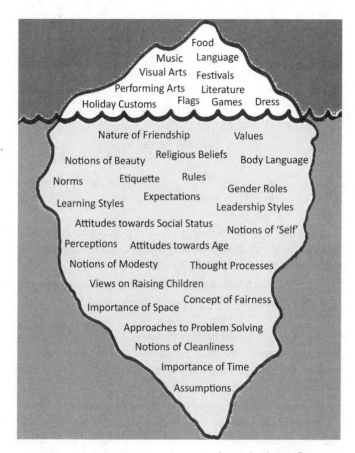

Image by James Penstone

Stepping Up, Stepping In: Facilitating For Freedom

by Makani Themba

They asked her to midwife—as if this was birthing. It wasn't. There was no single being created, no little life to tend. It was a meeting. They just found themselves without words for what they were trying to create. And there she was, femme and willing to hold them in a strict economy of words—speaking only when it was absolutely required.

As we, bright beings of transformation, wrest facilitation away from the western canons of management, masculinity, and efficiency, we can find ourselves rooting our work in an idea that also denies our magic; a version of facilitation "in the feminine" in which, in the service of support, we can cede our knowing.

We hold space. We invite. We offer. And although we should reject modalities that do not give our people space to dream, choose, express, decide, we should also reject those that deny us, as facilitators, the space to bring *our* wisdom and magic into the room in the service of progress.

Facilitation in the context of collective liberation means that you are not simply a bystander in service to the "space." You are a comrade in collective-conspiring with the same need for justice, for forward motion toward a world where we all thrive. Although many groups say that they want to facilitate liberatory space, they also operate under a belief in "objectivity" that makes it difficult to respect their own comrades as facilitators. They want an "outside" "expert"—not just to free up time and space for members but because they think of holding space as something we do *for* and not *with* each other. These tightly held notions of facilitator as external observer are why so much of my support work with other facilitators is helping them navigate how to effectively operate in *their own* organization.

Years ago, I made the decision to step away from facilitation in the western mode that required my silence and prohibited my sharing content (versus process) expertise. I called what I did "strategy support" in order to avoid debates with those still enmeshed in the western idea of the facilitator as "objective" observer. Bottomline, it is about having the agreement that everyone in the room gets to "speak a word" if forward motion requires it.

Many of our movements are in desperate need of, uh, *movement*. We can get caught up in meeting process as the sole container for how we work together, for how we practice democracy. It is the difference between understanding the meeting as one of many tools for clarifying values, work, and roles and the meeting as "the work" itself. Hint: if you are organizing and the only thing you can invite your people to is a meeting, this might be an indicator of where you are on this continuum. It is sad how many groups never quite get to do change work in the world together, to learn together, make mistakes together, and most importantly, make a difference together.

It was their eighth meeting in three years. Everyone was so busy maintaining and moving their individual organizations that finding the time for "third body" work—the work of building the relationships and strategy between their organizations—was stalled. It seemed to mock them and drain their energy. It became a thing to avoid. No one wanted reminders of what they didn't know how to do. She stood there asking questions, hoping she'd find one that would unlock the malaise, the fear, the stuckness.

The discomfort, and even unwillingness, to intentionally face what we do not know in change work has dogged organizing for decades. There are folk working to build out large, multiracial coalitions with no prior experience. Groups in their separate corners starting and starting and starting things without much inquiry because we have somehow internalized the idea that change work, like most of the work we associate with people of color, comes "naturally" without study or training. As facilitators, our work can perpetuate these myths when we act as if everything that needs to be discerned will happen in the gathering without much preparation, study, or knowledge.

What would it look like to develop a framework for how we facilitate where intentional learning and strategy development are built in? Here are four ideas to help get the conversation started.

1. **Mapping assets and experience as part of the process.** Of course, we want to value all kinds of experience, but let us do a better job of at least knowing what our people know, what they are passionate about, things they've tried, and what they've learned so that we can build on it. This could take the form of additional survey questions, a structured biographical essay (written, or in video format for folk with writing and/or reading challenges), or a storytelling project. The key is to do it well enough in advance of convenings so that the information can be used to strengthen how and what we discuss.

2. **Share our study resources.** There are so many formations on parallel paths, trying to answer many of the same questions. We need to pool and co-curate the resources we generate and the popular education processes we are learning/innovating to support our people in engaging these ideas. As facilitators, we can ask our comrades how they study, what they study, and where and how they share these resources. We can also better integrate systems for learning and reflection into how we support the work.

3. **Map and track emergent questions, no matter how seemingly simple.** Sometimes, we can be ashamed of our questions. We hold them in silence because we are worried about being judged. Creating an environment that welcomes all to raise what they don't know and develops concrete activities to address their questions is an important part of movement

facilitation. We are here to build with one another, to deepen trust, to sharpen our skills and analysis so that we build the individual and collective power to transform the world. Inquiry, interrogation, and co-learning are all major components of how this happens. Another critical element is, in spite of conditions, getting our folk to *allot enough time* for discussion.

4. **Be rigorous in our study of *how* folk have approached/ are approaching the work.** Although we can step up study in every aspect of our work, perhaps our understanding is most underdeveloped around the practice of *how* we move work forward. How did we decide? What did the organizing look like? What did we have to learn and master to get that done? Did we start out trying this or was this practice the result of learning and adjustments? These are just some of the questions that help us get a clearer picture of how good work gets done. Unfortunately, little is written about how we do things. We mostly unearth it in "interviews"—impromptu conversations at the bar or the all too brief panel presentations where the story is pared down to eight minutes. There has been, is, and will be amazing work going on and, as facilitators, we often get a beautiful "bird's eye" view. When appropriate and principled, we should share the stories we know to help move the work forward. We can also support folk in this area by ensuring that they develop timelines and task lists that include how they document and share their learning.

We are living in high stakes times. There is no one to spare. There is no bystanding. In the immortal words of Butterscotch, "We are all what we've got." And it will be important to bring all of who we are and what we've got into the work—especially our experience, expertise, heart, and memory—so that we can get further, faster, together. Working in a spirit of honest inquiry, we can co-create spaces that are alive with our wisdom and our wondering. It will take nothing less to get free.

*
**

What Is Principled Struggle?

with N'Tanya Lee

A few years ago I was cofacilitating a high stakes meeting with N'Tanya Lee (and Makani Themba), and this question was asked. Not out of the blue—we'd been in a bit of a knot as a group. The group was composed of a dozen of the key leaders from Black movement organizations at the national level with key local movement leaders from the midwest, deep south, coasts. They knew they were stuck—the facilitation team for this small group was three Black women deep. The quicksand was around how to struggle, and a few people had said either that they wanted to engage in principled struggle, or that the way another group was showing up was not principled. So, "what is principled struggle?" was a very relevant and timely question, one of those moments where some bit of language we have been using as common tongue gets pulled under the microscope and examined in ways that can change the direction of a movement.

While Makani and I reflected on how to get the group back on track, N'Tanya posted a big sheet of paper on the wall and wrote in block letters across the top: **Principled Struggle**. N'Tanya has been a long-term organizer, helping communities understand the relevance and practice of socialism. What she offered was a framework rooted in Marxism for principled struggle.

I wish I could show you the faces of the organizers in that room, softening, mouths opening in that ah that says, "Oh I understand this. I can do this."

I found the framework so useful, so compelling, that I brought it into every Black and multiracial space I entered afterwards, each time watching people relax as they came to understand that we would not hide from conflict in this space, that we trusted ourselves to hold it, and that we would only hold what was appropriate to hold.

So, here is my expanded version of what N'Tanya wrote:

We struggle for the sake of deepening our collective understanding and getting to greater unity. We are not battling just to be right, to make others wrong. We are not trying to colonize the collective space with our ideas or pontification. We want to understand each other, and fundamentally we want to build a bigger *we* from which to advance our movements towards justice.

Be honest and direct—while holding compassion. Often we are comfortable doing one or the other. We can be honest and direct without care. In fact, this has become a lot of social media culture, to be honest and direct in a state of constant attack, shrinking or correcting others. Or we can hold so much compassion that it feels like an act of harm to just tell or hear the truth. What we aim for instead is a balance—to be able to speak the truth to other human beings, attuned to the impact, and in a spirit of moving towards shared understanding and unity.

Take responsibility for your own feelings and actions. Part of how power is removed from people is convincing us we do not have it. And part of stepping into collective power is recognizing that you have power, you have agency. In our movements, we can default to a place of feeling like others should be held accountable for every feeling that we have, forgetting that we can each learn how to shift our internal state, name our needs, and be intentional about how we bring our feelings into shared space. It is incredible to be in a group of sophisticated organizers who are able to name feelings that the collective needs to deal with, and orient themselves towards a larger call.

Seek deep understanding. Ask questions! Read the article! Ask and read before you bring a critique! Do not assume that everything you say is instantly and fully understood by others, and do not assume that what you are hearing is necessarily what the speaker intends. Especially when it appears that there is a vast difference in worldview, or a new proposal or piece of information. Think of it as if you're online—don't comment based on the headline. Click through, read the article. Ask the speaker what they intend, ask for clarity instead of asserting it.

Consider that this may or may not be the container to hold all that you need to bring. We are always our whole selves, but that does not mean that every space is the appropriate place for every need we have to be met, or idea to be heard. Some containers are focused on action, some are focused on the development of theory, some are organizing campaigns, some are spaces of alliance, some are political home. Political home is the place where your whole self should feel held, made room for, adapted for, and grown. In almost every other space, it is important to understand the goals and objectives, the focus. Make sure that what you have to bring is appropriate to the container.

Side conversations, or one on ones, should help us get better understanding, not check out. We all need room to vent, to process, to get clear on what isn't working. But when we are trying to grow deeper unity, we shouldn't use the side conversations to sow dissent, disrespect the process, or organize participants away from unity or principled critique. **One great test is to ask yourselves, "Could I bring the essence of this conversation back to the group?"** A critique that is never voiced in the full group is not given the power to truly shape the future of the work.

Principled Struggle

(via N'Tanya Lee)

we struggle for the sake of deepening our collective understanding & getting to greater unity!

be honest and direct—while holding compassion

take responsibility for your own feelings & actions

seek deeper understanding (ASK, READ, 1ST)

consider that this may or may not be the container to hold what you need to bring

side convos / one-on-ones ⟶ should help us get better understanding, NOT check out. test: could I bring the essence of this convo back to the group?

To Give Your Hands To Freedom, First Give Them To Grief

by Malkia Devich-Cyril

Don't surrender your loneliness
So quickly.
Let it cut more deep.
Let it ferment and season you
As few human
Or even divine ingredients can.
Something missing in my heart tonight
Has made my eyes so soft,
My voice
So tender,
My need of God
Absolutely
Clear.
—Hafiz

There are consequences to denying grief.

The morning my mother died was cold, dark, and the snowfall outside was frenzied and piling high. I'd put my headphones on in the night to block the loud hiss and moan of my mother's oxygen machine. I was tired. Less than six months after founding the

Youth Media Council, which would later become the organization MediaJustice, doctors told my sister and me that sickle cell anemia, a fatal genetic blood disorder, was finally and actively taking my mother's life. I was tired. For three years following the end-stage diagnosis I flew home from Oakland to Brooklyn for one week every month to relieve my sister of caregiving duties. It was hard work, washing and feeding and cleaning up after a stubborn dying adult whose own body had paved the way for mine, whose own hands had washed and fed and cleaned up after me. I was tired.

Just a few inches away, as I slept, my mother died at the young age of fifty-nine. The memory is fifteen years old as I write this, and cloudy. I remember the small pink pool of blood that had spilled from the corner of her mouth. That her legs were barely covered by animal print pajamas that didn't even reach her ashen ankles. Just beside the stark memory of the rough, ashen patch of elbow jutting from my mom's blue t-shirt is my memory of time thick and muddled, moving so slow that I could hear my heart beating in my throat. While it was her towering love and brilliant rage that pressed me into being, my mother looked fragile in death, small, her deep brown skin scarred like that of a battered child.

As I stood above my mother's deathbed, her body curved like a crescent moon, my hands a sickled semi-circle around her, a feeling of abject failure gurgled in my throat. I couldn't swallow it. I couldn't spit it out. In that moment, it seemed the world could pass right through me, that's how invisible, how spiritually thin I felt. My mother's big, complicated life had ended. I didn't know if she had been afraid, or what her last moments of life were like. I only knew that my mom, a single mother and a leader in the Harlem Chapter of the Black Panther Party, had passed to me all of my politics and seeded in me all the things that I am, good and bad. It was my mother who believed me when I told her someone was hurting me, when no one else did. When I came out as queer at the age of twelve, my mother became a parent leader in the movement for queer and trans rights. My mother stood for me when no one else did, and she died while I slept. On my watch. That was my singular thought. That guilt, the incongruence between working daily to heal the world, but being unable to save my mother's life was powered by the illusion of my control over life and death—an entire worldview centered on my failure.

I had already helped seed a half dozen groups and even more ideas. I was one of the leaders diversifying and forging an emerging media justice sector. I was making the kind of difference I had always wanted to make. I could coordinate campaigns and build communities, I could navigate wins and losses, with order, plans, brains. That's what I thought. I could control this.

At my mother's bedside, there were decisions to be made. People to call. In the days and weeks that followed, there would be legal papers to sign, a memorial to organize, a will to execute, debts to settle, taxes to file, clothes to pack and give away, my mother's brownstone to manage. But, on the morning that I woke to her death, it didn't matter that I had previously managed staff, planned major actions, or trained dozens of leaders. Death sucked up all the oxygen in the room, left me breathless and confused. In that state, I forgot everything I was supposed to do. I called the police when I should have called the hospice program. I called an ex-lover with whom I was in an unhealthy relationship instead of calling any of the dozen friends that had been helping me during this time. When anyone tried to touch my mother's cold body, I yelled at them. When my seven-year-old niece cried, confused, I didn't know what to do. Guilt at my helplessness filled my every pore, and robbed me of the agency and grounded presence the moment required. Things were out of control.

Instead of surrendering to grief's momentum, I backed away from it with everything I had. I continued to run away for the next five years. I ran into nicotine, into alcohol, into sex. I ran into drama and into conflict. But more than anything, more than everything, I ran headfirst into my job. I worked all through the night, at bars and at conferences. Everywhere, all the time.

During that first five years after my mother's death I entered what poets and psychologists alike have dubbed the "dark night of the soul," a stage in personal development when a person undergoes a difficult and significant transition, and the previous frameworks like identity, relationship, career, habit, or a belief system that previously gave life meaning no longer do. Author and grief activist Francis Weller suggests that while this dark night can often look like depression, it is actually the deformation of personality that occurs when oppression forces individuals, communities, and generations to carry grief as a solitary burden. He says the psyche knows we are not capable of handling grief in isolation. Whether the message is coming from the nation-state, your employer, or family and friends, when the message is "Get over it. Get back to work," people frequently try to numb themselves to cope with the discomfort of loss and the feelings of extreme deprivation and isolation that can follow. Weller suggests that addiction acts as an anesthetic mechanism to try and cope with intolerable conditions and emotions.

In August 2005, six months after my mother died beside me, Hurricane Katrina hit the Southern Gulf Coast, killing almost two thousand people in the storm and the flooding that followed. It felt like the Category 5 tropical storm hit the collective Black body with extreme prejudice and force. I couldn't go to New Orleans where bodies were being fished from the water. I didn't go help my comrades, provide emergency support, or do any of the things I would have otherwise done. I was suffering, and I was deeply ashamed.

By the time I was thirty years old, I had quite an intimate relationship with death and dying. My mother's death wasn't my first major loss, it just had the greatest impact. I had grown up in Bedford-Stuyvesant, Brooklyn, in the 1980s when Black bodies were felled like great trees, cut down by bullets, by intimate violence, by accidents and disease. I knew death, but I did not recognize the grief sitting, unmoving, in my skin. I grew heavy with it, angry, defensive, and I would not learn to drink from the well of grief until a decade later, when I suffered the second extreme loss of my life.

As is the way with major loss, my mother's death hallowed me, knocked me to my knees, and emptied me until there was nothing left but holy ground. It was in that tender and sacred state that I reconnected with Alana Devich, the queer Black femme from my college alma mater who would become my best friend, then my soulmate, and then my wife. I never thought we would get married, neither one of us was looking for that. But, from our first hot and awkward date in a smoky bar, we were guided by a higher magic, an alchemy that led us right to our wedding day three years later, where we shared our vows with about a hundred friends and family members, and hundreds more on Livestream. With or without state sanction, the words "til death do us part" were a promise I could easily make, in part because I was experiencing an unparalleled love, but also because I was certain that the world had already taken from me all it was going to take. I was ecstatic, finally. I had done my work. Loss had ravaged me but it had not won. Alana's quiet, stubborn quirk was a kind of genius to me. It made her the most insightful and wittiest person I had ever met. Her kindness was threaded through with a streak of melancholy, a freshly tendered gratitude that saw and delighted in everything; even me. Especially me. It may be the reason that when I put my cheek on her cheek and asked her to marry me, she didn't hesitate. She said yes. Even when I asked her again and again. She said yes and I was ready.

The year after our wedding was a blissful one. We traveled. Made plans to move from our junior one bedroom to a larger place with room for our future. We talked about buying a house. And so, it was a heart-wrenching shock when an oncologist walked into the office where we sat, arms around each other, and diagnosed Alana with an incurable end-stage gastro-esophageal cancer that had already invaded her liver, lungs, esophagus, bones. We cried in the doctor's office. We sat, stunned, and explained that this couldn't be right because we had just gotten married only one year ago. The doctor cried. We held hands. Alana said she wanted to fight, and, oh, we did. I don't know if two people have ever fought so hard for anything. Ever. As we worked our way through crisis after crisis, through twelve rounds of fifty-six-hour chemotherapy infusions, weekly IV hydration, frequent emergency hospitalizations, surgery and rehab, I continued to work as executive director of MediaJustice. Fundraising. Staff meetings. Human relations. Strategic Campaigns. I admit, it almost broke me. My wife, of whom I will forever be in constant awe, fought an exhaustive two-year battle against a painful, disabling, and debilitating cancer. And still, after everything, I found myself once again standing at a deathbed holding in my arms a woman I loved more than life itself. Though we had planned for this and built an incredible grief community, Alana was far too young and alive for death. I was in a state of shock. I couldn't accept it. Alana Devich Cyril, a woman who brought me closest to my truest self, had also brought me face to face with sacred death. She died peacefully at the young age of forty-two years old in my arms, at home. A part of me died that day too.

> There are things
> the kind of things that shatter a life
> collapse it, stomach to back
> Till the three dimensions it once was
> now fit, flat onto the page.

I'd spent the five years after my mother's death becoming a driven and overworked executive movement leader. I tried desperately to fill the hollow that grief had carved into my life by seeking familial connections with co-workers with whom I bonded over our shared history of trauma and loss. Though I was rooting around in the dark after the loss of my mother, trying to find my way, a small light was on. I joined the community that would become generative somatics and, over that decade, off and on, founder Staci Haines and others taught me practices that ultimately helped me integrate my traumatic loss. In those years, I led my organization to win national campaigns that impacted the lives of hundreds of thousands of people. I helped to build a new media justice and digital rights social justice sector. At times, I did so in ways that didn't center the dignity in myself and others. I learned the hard-won lesson that grief demands its due, and it will take by force what is not freely given.

But this journey through what experts call "complicated grief," in which the bereaved person experiences debilitating feelings of extreme loss that don't improve or integrate over time, is what revealed to me this truth: That in order to give my heart to love and my hands to freedom movements, I had to attend to first understand and attend to grief.

The Five Gates of Grief

So, how do we bring ourselves to grief in ways that nurture agency, accountability, and action? Developing a shared understanding of what we mean by grief is a good place to start. Cheryl Espinosa Jones, a grief counselor, author, and the host of *Good Grief Radio* at VoiceAmerica, explained to me during an informal interview that grief is any response to loss. While grief is most often associated with sorrow, anyone who has lost someone they love knows sorrow is not the whole of grief. Grief also includes great joy and gratitude. Espinosa Jones offered that we can experience grief in many ways, on a spectrum, and that despite some old ways of thinking about grief as moving in stages, grief actually moves in disordered, contextual cycles. The goal of grief work isn't to get rid of grief, but to move closer and closer to it.

Similarly, Francis Weller, grief activist and author of the book *The Wild Edge of Sorrow: Rituals of Renewal and the Sacred Work of Grief,* suggests that to move closer to our grief, we must each enter into an apprenticeship with sorrow. To that end, he outlines five gates to grief, or, five doors through which grief enters our lives.[1]

The first gate of grief, and perhaps the most obvious, is the principle that everything we love, we lose. Integrating this fundamental understanding into our lives and into our organizations can change the relationship of activists and organizers to loss, as we lean into the dynamic and immutable truth of change. Change is life's only inevitability. Loss can be a natural form of change, but even when it is traumatic or brought about by inequality and the concentrations of hierarchical power that force an imbalance of loss upon us, acknowledging the dynamic relationship between loss and love is an essential ingredient for movement leadership.

Weller's second gate of grief is those "places that have not known love." He describes these starved places as "the places within us that have been wrapped in shame and banished to the furthest shores of our lives." These are the wild impulses cut out of us as children and

---

1.   Francis Weller, *The Wild Edge of Sorrow: Rituals of Renewal and the Sacred Work of Grief* (Berkeley: North Atlantic Books, 2015).

denied us as adults. The boundless joy, the erotic, the imagination. These are the parts of ourselves we have learned to rein in, or worse, to hold with disgust and contempt. Each of us seeks to be whole, but if we see these parts of ourselves outside of what Weller calls the "circle of worth," how can we grieve what we deny has been lost?

The *third gate of grief* is what Weller calls "the sorrows of the world." Undocumented children detained. Millions of people incarcerated. The poverty and inequality that engorges a global ruling class. The discrimination and violence endured by queer, transgender, and disabled bodies. The police violence that disproportionately ends Black lives. The human rights abuses that create conditions of subjugation and oppression in every country in the world. Loss upon loss. This is the gate at which we acknowledge the universal nature of suffering. In Buddhist practice, the Four Noble Truths assert that suffering is human, but through centered action and long-term practice we can use everything at our disposal to move it aside, and gain freedom.

In a death-dealing culture marked by widespread suffering, many activists equate grief with trauma. Trauma manifests as a range of responses to a deeply distressing or disturbing event that overwhelms an individual's ability to cope, causes feelings of helplessness, diminishes one's sense of integrity and self, as well as one's ability to feel a full range of emotions and experiences. Some losses are traumatic, and we call that traumatic loss. Grief always occurs after trauma, but trauma does not always have to follow loss. In a more just world, more losses would simply be a natural balancing, a season with which we could be in dynamic relationship.

Weller's *fourth gate to grief* is what we expected and did not receive. Divorce, separation, and other relationship losses are common at this gate. But this is not simply interpersonal, this is also organizational and political. When cancer killed my wife Alana, after a years-long transition, I left my job of twenty years. While the organization I founded was left in the very capable hands of an insightful, strategic movement leader, the structures and systems I built were infused with my previous complicated grief. I didn't feel supported, and I don't think I am alone in that feeling. Part of how we must meet grief requires that we both strengthen the infrastructure of movements so they live up to our expectations as we grieve, and that we adjust our unrealistic expectations of what movements and organizations and leaders can heal in us. Our collective disappointment with the imperfections of the movements we build are a reflection of our refusal to grieve the truth that perfection is impossible. Blame refuses grief's complexity and wisdom. Blame forces our eyes in the wrong direction. When blame appears as a pattern, it is in fact a reactionary habit that grows out of society's ritual denial of grief.

Weller's fifth gate to grief is ancestral grief. Our losses are generational. A relatively new concept in public health is the "Historical Trauma Theory." The idea here is that groups of people historically subjected to long-term, mass trauma—colonialism, slavery, war, genocide—exhibit a higher prevalence of disease, even several generations after the original trauma occurred, with the additional challenge of damaged cultural identity. When a population experiences a forced loss of language, land, nation-state, humanity, and sovereignty, and basic rights, coupled with an enormous loss of life, the effects of those collective traumatic losses can be felt for generations and cause specific epigenetic changes, according to researcher Michelle Sotero.[2]

In a 2004 study that surveyed adult Indigenous people who had children, researchers developed something called the Historical Loss Scale.[3] The study found that though Indigenous participants were generations removed from specific historical traumas inflicted upon their respective communities, 36 percent had daily thoughts about the loss of traditional language in their community, and 34 percent experienced daily thoughts about the loss of culture. Additionally, 24 percent reported feeling angry regarding historical losses, and 49 percent provided they had disturbing thoughts related to these losses.

---

2. See Michelle Sotero, "A Conceptual Model of Historical Trauma: Implications for Public Health Practice and Research," *Journal of Health Disparities Research and Practice* 1, no. 1 (Fall 2006).

3. Les B. Whitbeck, Gary W. Adams, Dan R. Hoyt, and Xiaojin Chen, "Conceptualizing and Measuring Historical Trauma Among American Indian People," *American Journal of Community Psychology* 33, no. 3/4 (June 2004).

As humans, we are hardwired for the fact that death is a natural part of life. While loss is deeply uncomfortable, we can learn to adapt to the natural phenomenon of loss. But when structural inequalities produce major and secondary losses, leading to widespread collective grief, death is out of balance with life. Individual and collective, repeated and generational, traumatic loss stacked on top of existing natural loss. We must tear down the systems, institutions, and narratives that engineer death, fuel it and simultaneously distract us from it. This essential rebalancing act is the charge of twenty-first-century social justice movements.

To be Black, Indigenous, or a member of any oppressed class in America is to know traumatic loss. But as we strip away the chains of nation-state to become a true patriot to the nation that has not yet been born—the one beyond national borders and prison bars, the one forged in the fire of a deep, abiding love with an economy steeped in dignity and rights—we can come to know a richly resilient grief rather than a desperate, starving one.

To Shift the Balance of Power, Grief is a Skill We Need

Death is not the burden. Inequality and the violent imbalance of power is.

"Interregnum" is a term given to the uncertain period between stable governments when anything might happen: civil unrest, war between nations, the rise of militias and other warlords, power vacuums, and succession wars. When these periods of instability end, the dust settles, and the victors restabilize the empire, there is often a new geography, new borders, new lines of delineation. In 1929, the Italian writer and political theorist Antonio Gramsci was incarcerated in a fascist prison, writing about what he considered to be a new interregnum, a Europe that was tearing itself apart. He wrote of anticipated war between nations, civil unrest, and repeated changes in the lines of geographic possession. "The crisis consists precisely in the fact that the old is dying and the new cannot be born; in this interregnum a great variety of morbid symptoms appear."[4] Or, in its more common phrasing, "The old

---

4. Antonio Gramsci, *Selections from the Prison Notebooks*, ed. and trans. Quintin

world is dying, and the new world struggles to be born: now is the time of monsters."

In the twenty-first century, our cities smell more and more like fire. As the old world dies and a new one struggles to be born, the morbid symptoms of which Gramsci spoke are showing their monstrous faces and spreading their deliberate pain like a bruise across the skin of the planet. White supremacy, capitalism, and patriarchy are ideological and structural systems that both beget and reject grief, fuel destructive violence, and keep communities clinging to the old world, clinging to how things were instead of imaging what it could be, clinging to the ideology of control. At-tempting to control life is often an attempt to escape death, from which there is no escape. These systems radically distort our rela-tionship to death.

But death belongs; it's not the burden. Death is a natural part of every life cycle. Our bodies will die. Our organizations will die. Our movements will die. Likewise, the specific conditions that op-press our families and communities will also come to an end. End-ings are not to blame. Loss is simply an element of change.

Change is the heartbeat of social movement. But, on either side of change is loss. Coping with loss is a skill that should be taught as fundamental to social movement leadership. Reimag-ining the world requires that we release the parts of the system and ways of being that are ready to die, and mourn the destructive losses that we could not control, despite our best efforts. As we bear witness to increasingly visible ecological destruction book-ended by the crumbling decay of late-stage high-tech capitalism and the violence of an authoritarian state infected with resurgent white nationalism, we must transform the pandemic fear, power-lessness, and exhaustion of this century into a pandemic joy, rooted in empowered grief. Our movements for equity and human rights depend on it.

Something is dying, and we are desperate for something new to be born.

We can feel it, quivering with hope at the edge of a century. It

Hoare and Geoffrey Nowell-Smith (London: Lawrence & Wishart, 1971), 276.

is a firecracker dancing across a night sky. A languid score of Black music moving effortlessly in the street. The fires lit call to us like beacons across state lines, a collective grievance demarcating what was from what will be. Here. Now. Grounded grief is a vaccine against the morbid conditions bred by white supremacy, a patriarchy that has distorted our families and relationships, a concentration of wealth that has disconnected us from nature and directed everything brilliant and beautiful to profit. Only through the compassion and loneliness and love inherent in grief can we forge a world out of the fire that will not replicate ancient hierarchies, nor replace old gods with new ones that are just as arrogant and just as punitive.

On either side of change is loss. To reimagine and reshape the world, grief is a skill we need.

Grief In Action

What becomes possible when movements are brought more healthfully to grief, and what can we do to support leaders, organizations, and movements to get there?

Cheryl Espinosa Jones offered me four steps for moving through grief, which I interpreted as an offering not only for individual activists and leaders, but also for organizations and social movements as a whole.

Feel the loss fully. We can trust grief. Espinosa Jones makes it plain, "Grief knows what it's doing." Like the soma in general, grief is wise and ancient and knows what to do. When we interrupt grief's processes, or ignore them, it can lead to apathy, addiction, and unhealthy forms of anger. What loss hates most is to be ignored.

Yet, for centuries, systems of racial, economic, and gender hierarchy have disenfranchised the grief of people of color, women, children, disabled people, queer and trans communities, and the poor. Dominant narratives about grief have turned gaslighting into an art form, convincing us that it is safer to deny grief than to feel it. At every turn, we are persuaded that grief is a wild, unacceptable emotion that must be handled, managed, overwritten, and hidden. We are pressured by political and even physical force to prioritize productivity over personal wellbeing, to seek eternity over embodied presence, even as we live through the most traumatic losses.

For each Black life taken by police or interpersonal violence, how many spouses, siblings, children, or parents had sufficient bereavement leave? What would happen if Black diasporic communities were to fully embody the losses of land, culture, and freedom emerging from chattel slavery? Would agency or apathy be the result if immigrant communities could steep in the loss of land, language, and family? Would Indigenous communities across the globe have more or fewer negative health outcomes if there were space to feel and then transform the grief of genocide? As we seek to breathe a new world into being, being an effective changemaker demands the right and power to feel our losses rather than escape them. We must give our grieving bodies what they need, individually and collectively.

How do you give a grieving system what it needs? First and foremost, stop conflating health and productivity. Stop giving positive feedback when staff immediately return to work, appear less emotional, and/or don't ask for appropriate accommodations following a major loss. The systems of inequality we seek to transform reject what Espinosa Jones calls "a relational culture." Meaning: a culture of noticing and acknowledgment. Violently enforced inequality makes truth, reconciliation, reparations, and accountability impossible. But noticing grief allows us to make an assessment about what it is we need. Becoming aware of grief gives us more choices about how to respond to grief, and opens up possibilities to approach grief not only with compassion for self and others, but also with joy. Joy is not the opposite of grief. Grief is the opposite of indifference. Grief is an evolutionary indicator of love—the kind of great love that guides revolutionaries.

Seek solace and comfort. As we expand a broad awareness of grief, we learn to approach our own grief and the grief of others without judgment. We practice the art of accompaniment without casting any part of ourselves out. Buddhist practices like meditation and its teachings on impermanence and the nature of suffering can help. Denying grief denies humanity. Yet, becoming aware of one's own grief, reaching out for professional or peer support, and owning your grief journey can open your awareness until you see grief you didn't even realize was there.

When faced with traumatic grief, professional support is an important intervention. Most hospice programs host free bereavement groups and counseling open to the community regardless of your health insurance. But, since grief itself is a natural process, seeking or building peer support is equally valid. In community, we can move together, take action that can help metabolize sorrow and transform grief, releasing impossible goals such as eliminating grief.

Instead, during times of massive collective loss, let us rebuke apathy by re-imagining social justice organizations and formations as vehicles to metabolize and transform grief into agency. This requires resilient infrastructure and embodied methodology. Resilient infrastructure may include special funds and referral lists that support staff healing, extended bereavement leave policies, and the ability to cross-train staff to share responsibilities and increase organizational redundancy and support staff boundaries. At the end of the day, the question is whether your leaders and staff have the skills to recognize grief and the resources to respond when it appears.

As societies or social movements, we must develop resilient adaptations that increase the elasticity of our responses to loss. Otherwise, our adaptations can morph into a traumatized response that relies heavily on traumatic bonds and decreases the strategic effectiveness and staying power of social movement organizations and leaders.

Religions prescribe practices to manage grief, and movements need to as well. To be aware of grief and to act on it individually is not enough. When social movements have neither the infrastructure nor leadership to enable the mass metabolizing of grief, they fracture under the weight of it, just like people do. If we could expand the social infrastructure for grief beyond hospice and faith, consider the kind of democratic social movements our civil society would give birth to?

Find inspiration. In the Civil Rights and Black Power/Third World Liberation movements of the 1960s, organizations and campaigns used song, poetry, and other art forms as a means to support the transformation of grief into a wise protagonism and active agency. Though our movements may be secular, they are in no less need of song and ritual. Art in all its forms allows grief to reveal us, gives sorrow words, deepens our gratitude with grief's weight, reminds each of us that only those who grieve profoundly can love deeply—and from loving another, grow our *agape* love for the world. That's why I launched the Pandemic Joy Community, a completely volunteer weekly online gathering, where I and approximately forty others meditate, pour libations, sing, and testify. It is why my wife would step out into the full moon light, or pull tarot cards at the new moon. It is why my mother played Billie Holiday at full volume and read poems to my sister and I on the floor of Liberation Bookstore in Harlem, NY.

Take action from this place of grounded grief. In our conversation, Espinosa Jones reminded me that an individual's psychology can heal by finding the courses of action that match one's felt need, but there are no skipped steps. Sitting with discomfort is always first, followed by connection and inspiration—but at the end of the day, we need action to metabolize grief, and transform our material and cultural conditions. Metabolized grief can power deep and lasting change infused with profound joy, while unmetabolized grief becomes an almost insurmountable barrier to it.

In the book *The Prophet*, Khalil Gibran writes, "Your joy is your sorrow unmasked. And the selfsame well from which your laughter rises was oftentimes filled with your tears. And how else can it be? The deeper that sorrow carves into your being, the more joy you can contain."[5] In my life, grief and joy have been as dark and light, a mirror translating the same energy into different languages. When I lost my mother, I learned that life promises death. When I lost my soulmate, I learned that love promises loss.

Along my own journey, what surprised me most was the discovery that grief is not an enemy to be avoided. In fact, resisting grief led to my suffering, becoming intimate with grief led me to the lesson that grief and joy are inextricably linked. Though

5.   Khalil Gibran, *The Prophet* (New York: Knopf, 1962), 32.

generations of traumatic loss can become conflated with deformed expectations, standards, and culture, grief in all its forms has the potential to bring us closer to the truth of the world, to make us more tender and more filled with delight. It is from this new kind of gratitude, this pandemic joy, that we can risk together in action, in democratic decision making, in strategic vision. This is one part of liberation.

What if what is true for me is also true for you?

What if the answer is not to see grief as a weakness but as a strength?

What if we are not supposed to move away from grief, but to move closer to it?

What if the answer is not to make grief precious, requiring special treatment, but to understand it as normal and nutritious to individuals and equally transformative to social movements?

What if we saw grief as a path to greater tenderness, and understood that tenderness can bring greater strategic clarity?

What if vulnerability was the victory and a path to deeper satisfaction, effectiveness, creativity, and impact?

When we bring our fights to the watering hole of grief, our political systems, natural environment, economic frameworks, civil society, and culture all become living breathing memorials to what we have lost. What we have lost becomes found, witnessed, honored. In this way, all social justice and human rights work is a collective act of gloried mourning.

To have a movement that breathes, you must build a movement with the capacity to grieve.

*
**

An Invitation to Brave Space

by Micky ScottBey Jones

Together we will create *brave space*
Because there is no such thing as a "safe space"—
We exist in the real world.
We all carry scars and we have all caused wounds.
In this space
We seek to turn down the volume of the outside world,
We amplify voices that fight to be heard elsewhere,
We call each other to more truth and love.
We have the right to start somewhere and continue to grow.
We have the responsibility to examine what we think we know.
We will not be perfect.
This space will not be perfect.
It will not always be what we wish it to be.
But
It will be *our brave space together,*
and
We will work on it side by side

Audre Lorde said, "The true focus of revolutionary change is never merely the oppressive situations that we seek to escape, but that piece of the oppressor which is planted deep within each of us."[1]

We must confront oppressive situations that keep us in chains. One of the ways we confront oppression is to do the concentrated work of bravely facing what needs healing on the inside, which—in some strange dance of inner and outer work—is revealed as we are doing the work of dismantling the larger systems of oppression. It is a both-and proposition. Doing the work reveals more of the work to be done in us. The means are the ends—and if we simply confront the oppression "out there" (the white supremacist, capitalist, heteropatriarchal structures) and not "in here" (ourselves) and "in here" (our movement communities), we will only be creating more culturally familiar versions of the systems we say we want to dismantle.

This is some of what has surfaced for me while exploring the practice of inviting myself and others into creating *brave spaces*—brave space that we carry within and brave space that we practice with others. Spaces that are not just safe (which feels so fragile and precarious to maintain), but spaces that also encourage us to be very in touch with our needs and our energy, to give as we are able, to heal ourselves as we offer healing to each other and the world, and to practice in ways that open up possibilities of transformation.

Creating spaces that are safe is admirable, *and* our addiction to safety (I wonder sometimes if it's more about comfort, lack of conflict, or a desire to create *set it and forget it* containers) has at times devolved into long periods of agreement setting and developing a list of rules for every possible way of relating to one another, where the focus is more on the policing of tone, language, and surface level behavior that makes performative participation easier and vulnerable participation more difficult. The framework of inviting each other into brave spaces is, at its core, a baseline agreement to be in authentic working relationship. Its focus is on becoming skillful in navigating the messiness of different starting points, divesting from perfection, working at the speed of relationship,

---

1.   Audre Lorde, "Age, Race, Class, and Sex: Women Redefining Difference," in *Sister Outsider: Essays and Speeches* (Berkeley: Crossing Press, 1984/2007), 123.

attending to our own frustrations, and practicing accountability, transformative justice, repair, and even separation in generative ways that create more liberation in the midst of work, not just as a result of it.

One of the most lovely things about the words "brave space" is how different communities have adapted them for themselves, co-creating a way of talking about how they want to be together that works for them. And isn't that brave? It takes so much courage to try to create community over and over again, considering the human record. It is so brave to organize, strategize, and dream together in the middle of oppression and trauma that seems to be reinvented every generation. This invitation to brave space is just that, an invitation to work side-by-side in ways that open us up to more possibilities for how we build together.

We Keep Us Safe: Facilitating Safer Spaces

by Ejeris Dixon

There's a healthy debate in movement spaces about the role of the facilitator. Are we leading the meeting or guiding the meeting? How do we intervene in harmful, violent, or toxic dynamics? When do we intervene? Should we intervene?

I believe that a safer space is a space where we have constructed the culture and the conditions where people can intervene in harm and violence without needing support from the facilitator. And while I have co-created and facilitated these spaces, they are rare, specific, and magical.

Humbly offered, the following are some tips on how facilitators can navigate issues of harm, violence, conflict, and surveillance with movement groups.

Preparing to Facilitate: Safety and Security Considerations

Many facilitators use an assessment process, which can include interviews, surveys, or group conversations to better understand whom they are supporting. Even if you are a member of the group, an assessment can support you to better hold harm, conflict, and other challenging dynamics. Here are key ideas to explore prior to the meeting.

- **Why You?** Ask why you're facilitating the meeting. Why not someone else? What are the expectations of your facilitation? How are you seen and perceived by the group?

What formal and informal power do you have?

- **Understanding Context.** Learn the ecosystem that the group exists within. What issues do they work on? What campaigns are they leading? Who are their key collaborators? What kinds of opposition do they experience? Are they engaged in rapid response or other forms of high-pressure activities? What's the likelihood that they are under surveillance? What forms of oppression do their members experience? Have they had any recent interactions with police, FBI, DHS, or ICE? Does the group or its leaders have a lot of visibility? Have there been recent incidents of harm or violence? Who is in leadership? Who has power?

- **Unlocking Necessary Truths.** When people ask you to facilitate, the stories they *want* to tell you are often not as helpful as the stories they are ashamed to tell you. Create open, non-judgmental space for groups to talk about the accountability processes gone wrong, the security practices that aren't enacted, the person they're concerned is an informant, the member that they will never trust. Sometimes I tell them I've seen everything, made every "error," and it's easier when I know what I'm working with. Avoid shaming folks for having conflict, harm, abuse, or violence within their groups. This is common and unfortunately normal, and it gives you an opportunity to support the group in moving through these situations.

- **Safety and Security Structures.** Explore what the group's security culture and safety practices look like. Is there a safety team or an accountability committee that can be available while you're facilitating? Have there been trainings on intervening in violence or transformative justice? Are there people who can support folks who get triggered during the meetings? Are there rituals or healing practices that the group uses to navigate trauma, stress, or conflict? Are there location-based safety needs? Where are the exits? Where's the fire extinguisher? What's the nearest hospital? Where's the nearest precinct? Who should be contacted during an emergency? Depending on what exists, make sure to meet with the relevant point people ahead of time to get their support and to continue to understand the situations in which the group needs safety and security strategies.

During the Meeting: Facilitator Opportunities

- **Create a Culture of Intervention.** The work of creating a culture where people intervene starts before you arrive in the room. During your prep work with the group remind them that you are co-creating the space, and ask how they would like to intervene in a case of harm, violence, or conflict. Utilize meeting agreements that are from and familiar to the group whenever possible. Co-facilitate sections of the agenda with group members. Ensure that the agreements create space for participants to name harm, intervene, and "call each other in" during conflict. Also ensure that people consent to use the agreements in the first place.

- **Avoid Defensiveness.** Facilitators can feel like they have to have all the answers and we often don't. Sometimes people confuse facilitation with public speaking or training. Sometimes facilitators can abuse their power or cause harm. To create safer spaces sometimes the group will need to educate us. Therefore we must accept feedback with grace, even if it isn't given gracefully. This doesn't mean that facilitators shouldn't have boundaries, but sometimes out of embarrassment facilitators get defensive and exacerbate harm. Avoiding defensiveness also allows facilitators to assess if people are asking for a shift in the agenda or facilitation style, and whether that shift is possible. It also allows facilitators to understand whether the feedback is truly feedback, or a person who desires more power and visibility in the meeting.

- **Deep Listening.** Facilitation is a practice in deep listening, noticing and engaging with words, body language, facial expressions, vocal tone, and the energy within the space. As facilitators read the room and interpersonal dynamics, it's critical to be attentive and ask questions about what people need. Sometimes harm and conflict are a result of the group's needs not being met; people may need breaks, food, or the discussion may be too difficult for the time of day. Additionally, facilitators need to be precise and attentive when paraphrasing and summarizing participants' words. Misrepresenting a person's thoughts can feel minimizing and escalate a situation. It's also fine to just repeat what a person has said as opposed to summarizing.

- **Navigating Unknown Dynamics.** Despite the most thorough preparation, there's always a dynamic in the room that's unknown to the facilitator. Sometimes it's an abusive ex, a toxic boss, or people with deep and historic political disagreements in the same meeting. Sometimes people use phrases and code words to cause harm during a meeting. Non-verbal communication and the room's energy will almost always highlight that something is wrong. Facilitators can interrupt this by asking the room, "what's going on?" Or facilitators can check in with their point people to figure out what's happening, what interventions are needed, and what participants can hold versus what the facilitator can hold.

- **Interrupting Violence and Harm.** Facilitators should guide the group towards the goals of a meeting but not to the specific points of the agenda. This allows room to address harm and reduce harmful dynamics as they arise. Sometimes a person wants a group member removed based on past harm without knowing the specifics or context. And while we should believe survivors, people who cause harm also use this tactic. Usually a good place to start is to take a break, learn more about what happened, and see if there is a way to create more safety for the participant other than removal (e.g. can there be space between participants, can there be agreements, is there another break out happening that the other person can join?). If there are no other options, then consider separating folks and removing, if needed. Resist the urge to pivot roles into either becoming a mediator or de-escalator. No facilitator can effectively facilitate *and* practice violence intervention simultaneously. If verbal conflict ensues, interrupt it (if the group doesn't first), take a break, debrief the incident with the group, and collaboratively revisit the agenda, even if it means canceling the rest of that day's facilitation. If physical violence happens, get the group away from the people who are involved and physically separate folks from each other. When these issues are resolved, divide roles among group members to check on the individuals involved and see what's needed. Engage the group in holding harm and violence with you. Ideally there are de-escalators, safety team members, or an accountability team. If not, we start these practices in the moment, assigning roles, and deepening from that point onward.

- **Adhering to Security Agreements.** Most BIPOC groups who are organizing against state violence should assume that they are under some level of government surveillance. As a facilitator it's important to adhere to a groups pre-existing security practices and also exhibit security culture during facilitation. If there are suspected provocateurs or informants within the group, it's important to ask how the group is navigating this issue as opposed to calling folks out within the meeting. There are certain direct action, security, and strategy conversations that should not occur while cellphones and laptops are present. It's also critical for facilitators to request and ensure that meeting notes, agendas, and assessments are kept confidential, secure, and in encrypted formats—especially for targeted groups. If the group you're working with does not have security practices, facilitate a conversation on what security practices are needed for that meeting.

After the Meeting: Supporting Reconnection, Accountability, and Repair When Needed

- **Be Available.** Don't facilitate and disappear. Make time and space to debrief, reconnect, and address any issues, harm, or conflict that came up during facilitation. The group may need to create safety structures based on what happened during the meeting. If you have capacity to support the group in facilitating and intervening in conflict themselves, it can be a powerful way to leave the group with deeper safety practices.

- **Be Accountable**. If your facilitation contributed to harm, you may need to have some one-on-one conversations. There may be a need to apologize, make amends, or educate yourself on specific topics. Be an example of accountability in order to support group members in being accountable themselves.

*
**

Facilitation For Movement

by Paris Hatcher

In 2017, I was completing my fourth year as a full-time consultant and approaching almost fifteen years as an organizer. We were also two years into the Movement for Black Lives, and there had been an influx of need and demand for space holders, facilitators, and agenda designers. I wanted to meet the movement moment by providing a space for seasoned facilitators to hone the art and science of facilitation in order to have better meetings, clearer strategies, conflict dissipation, and stronger organizations and movements. Facilitation for Movement (FFM) was then created.

To being the design of FFM, I knew I wanted to get input from others, so I created a survey and posted it to Facebook. Over seventy people replied, sharing their insight on content, trainers, and more.

I was also doing my own research. I knew I wanted something more than an intro- and intermediate-level training. I wanted to go deeper and practice how to handle real life experiences that make our role as facilitator difficult and foreboding. In my research, I kept thinking about facilitators who inspired me. Facilitators who know how to hold the room with grace and space, who can move the agenda along or pause where necessary, who are knowledgeable and transparent and have you leaving the space feeling held and respected during your time. Two people came to my mind immediately: Inca Mohamed and Makani Themba!

I knew Inca Mohamed and Makani Themba would be a perfect and dynamic pairing and would be fantastic as the lead faculty for Facilitation for Movement. Inca and Makani have decades of experiences as nonprofit leaders, coaches, capacity builders. They come from different social justice movements and have vast experience working with a variety of organizations, leaders, and movements. Their facilitations styles are different and wildly complementary. I wanted to give participants and opportunity to see different ways of doing this work and that there is no one right way to do it.

So far, Facilitation for Movement has trained 150 facilitators in the art and a science of facilitation. Each session is at capacity, and the feedback we receive have been glowingly constructive. Now that we are a part of the largest social justice movement in our lifetime, we will need even more facilitators, space holders, and magic makers who will ensure that we are joyfully and thoughtfully navigating our way to liberation.

*
* *

Be Open to Experimenting

by Inca A. Mohamed

My facilitation is grounded in two things: my love and my compassion for people. My love is expressed as I strive to respect the dignity of each person in the room, and compassion is what I hold for the group in the room as they endeavor to accomplish a goal.

There is often a lack of clarity around what exactly that goal should be, and there is usually a range of commitment to any goal. As a facilitator, my role is to continuously support people to be in connection with their dignity and their power in order to actualize their vision.

I have been facilitating since I was fourteen years old—I am now sixty-six years old. It is very easy to get attached to what has worked for you in the past. Learning and experimenting with new approaches (if not conceptually new, at least new expressions of old concepts) is a key to keeping the excitement and passion alive as you walk into a room.

My new frontiers include deepening my understanding of integrating somatic practices into my work and opening my heart to addressing the need for healing in every room I enter. To work in this manner means that I cannot fear how I may be perceived and I must continuously remember what I was taught in my early career as a facilitator: trust that the people in the room have the answers, and be mindful that my job is not to get in the way, but to facilitate the surfacing of those answers.

FACILITATION

&

MEDIATION

What Is and Isn't Facilitation

Facilitate: To make easy, or easier. To facilitate movements for social and environmental justice is to support movement workers to bring about change.

People are complex! Organizations are complex, society is complex. The work of a facilitator is:

- To make it as easy as possible for complex people to do the complex work of shaping change together;
- To make it easier for a group or organization to understand where they are going and how to get there;
- To understand the culture they are trying to create, and give them a place to practice;
- To understand how their visions can be made manifest, and can shape their decisions in the here and now;
- To support solid, authentic organizing;
- And to use every space to dismantle colonial legacies of oppression and supremacy.

Facilitation isn't:

- Training/Teaching, lecture style. Training/Teaching is important, but distinct. As facilitators, we are (mostly) supporting groups to plan and practice movement activity together, not moving information from one mind into many minds. It helps if teachers have facilitation skills, and this book can help with that development, but fundamentally the content, strategy, direction, and data will come from the group. I generally aim for a 90/10 percentage rule in a room—that anything I have to say takes up no more than 10 percent of the time/space we have together, maximum. And that what I am sharing is agenda review, community agreements, summaries of what they navigated, questions they need to answer. While people often learn off our bodies, and I have definitely had people reflect that they learned from how I facilitated or spoke on something, my intention was not on teaching them, but on drawing forth the knowledge of many minds to align towards their common visions, intentions, plans, and obstacles.

- Manipulation. We are out of integrity if we use our power at the front of the room to make people do what we want, or think they should do. Related: facilitation is not glamouring. We are not casting a spell over people to make them do what we want.

- Organizing. At our best, we are facilitating organizers to collaborate, rather than divide and move against each other. Include our wisdom, yes, but if we cannot trust the group to move content, if we find ourselves pushing the Ouija board planchette, then we may not be in right relationship to the role or the group.

- Fixing the group. We aren't doctors or mechanics. We cannot just tell groups how to change.[1] We especially can't fix a problem that everyone tells us about privately but no one will mention in the actual meeting.

- Keeping groups calm. OR. Making groups happy.

- Leadership Development. We might be models that people are moved by and learn from, but unless we are explicitly hired to develop leaders as distinct work from facilitation, let's not attempt to shape and change the participants of a group, especially without their consent.

---

1. Believe me, I have tried! Confessions of a Recovering Control Freak.

- Performance. Don't put on a show of process, while the content has already been fully planned and processed. Facilitators are not penguin daddies, regurgitating processed nutrients into baby bird mouths. The process has to be authentic for the movement to be resilient and impactful.

- Diversifying. A facilitator is not responsible for bringing diversity or a different culture into a group. Be wary of a monocultural group, particularly where the culture is privileged, making requests like "sing us a song!" or "perform a poem" or turning to the facilitator for input that a missing population should be providing to the room.

Facilitation is a way of listening through and beyond the words being spoken, feeling for the current of longing underneath what can be spoken, listening through the fear, listening through the scar tissue: What is possible? What is the next step towards that possibility?

Facilitation is also about being the grounding presence in the room. Generally, don't party with the group. Don't get caught up in playing favorites or making the participants compete for your attention. Don't cross boundaries, and if, when, you do, be accountable and reestablish the lines. As the facilitator, you need to be a presence that the whole room can trust—trust to be present, on time, on purpose, trust to be a neutral person to whom anyone in the room can bring concerns, feedback, and ideas.

For this section of the book, the facilitation offers are organized by element. Within each element are Brief Thoughts (my attempt at a Tao of facilitation), some specific deep dives on approach or framework, and then suggested Practices for growing facilitation skills in that element.

What Is and Isn't Mediation

Mediation is holding space for tension and conflict to get expressed and addressed in a dispute, process, or relationship. Mediation happens when a pair or group of people cannot reach resolution between themselves and seek the support of a third party who is relatively neutral.

To mediate in a movement context is to intervene on organizational or interpersonal conflict, particularly conflict that is not generative, is distracting from our collective justice and liberation work, or that embodies regressive values we are trying to dismantle.

Mediation is one part of a transformative justice approach to the work. It asserts that, rather than moving into punitive measures like suspension, firing, calling out, public shaming, cancelation, or prison, there should be an attempt to hear each other, seek understanding, accountability, and interpersonal or community resolution. Mediation can help people find appropriate consequences, rather than reactionary punishments. Mediation helps to clarify power dynamics, make harmful patterns visible, and introduce the possibility that things could be made right, whole, and easeful.

Mediation is not:
- A surprise accountability process
- Guaranteed to help people get along like they used to
- An attempt to get one person to admit they were wrong

- Therapy for either or both parties
- A public process, or a process guaranteed to have a public outcome
- A stand-in for other healing work
- Appropriate for a situation in which ongoing physical, sexual, or psychological abuse is active

Mediation, the way I approach it, is an ancient human practice that happens in intimate space—I have done most of my mediating around a kitchen table, over tea, where people can see and feel each other. I imagine a lineage at my back, of oak trees and mycelium and grandparents, knowing this moment is temporary and survivable.

Mediation holds that the current moment is not the only moment, and that there are things we can do to decrease harm and increase respect and communication over time to change conditions and dynamics.

Mediation in my work often an extension of facilitation, a focusing and deepening of the attention brought to a single relationship, usually inside of a vast network of relationships. If one relationship in a system or network is dysfunctional or vulnerable, it means the whole system has a weak spot. And to strengthen it is not necessarily to mediate people towards friendship or recovery—a strong clear boundary can be the necessary reinforcement. For the structure of this book, the specifics of mediation are tied to emergent strategy elements after the facilitation teachings for that element. The deepest dive into my mediation methodology is in the transformative justice/resilience chapter: Kitchen Table Mediation.

Fractal Facilitation

Brief Thoughts about Fractal Facilitation

Very few things can actually happen in a large group. Almost nothing can happen in a large group without trust. Often, a group may want to have an involved, large-group conversation to build alignment. Without trust, these kinds of conversations can quickly become a space of performance and posturing. This can be a set-up.

It's harder to hold hate, cynicism, or judgment against someone when we know more of what they are going through. Create relationships between the people in the room. Let them ask and answer how they are—that can change what's possible in the room.

Part of our job as facilitators is to continuously assess for the trust in a group. This does not mean trust is a destination, or that we are searching for a perfection of trust. Trust begins as an internal measure of integrity—is there a felt and/or proven alignment between what is being said, what is done, what is felt? In a room, it helps to think of trust as a spectrum—is there adequate trust to move forward? If a group seems stuck in quicksand, ask if people are feeling trust in each other, in the process; ask what could increase trust, and give more time to the relationships.

People often think they need to take action when they actually need to build relationship. People often think they need process right at the moment when shared action would most help. Facilitation keeps people turning towards the most necessary next step.

Trust is built in small gestures and vulnerabilities. People build trust in mutual experiences—in pairs or small groups, where there is room for both/all people to show aspects of their true selves.

True self is the self we are when we aren't holding a particular role or representing a particular group—it's equal parts passion, skill, and calling. We are often our truest selves in solitude—as facilitators we want to make room for true selves to be in relationship with each other. We want to continually invite the selves that are unmasked, not performing and not repressing what is felt and known.

True selves extending trust to each other make up the most efficient working body, as less time is spent on posturing, repression, backdoor organizing, lies tangling and untangling, or doing work no one is actually excited about.

Most changes happen in small ways, and then build up. In our bodies, what seem to be sudden changes in health are often the final throes of long-term visible and invisible health struggles and choices. The same is true in our organizations. We need to pay attention to what we practice. Each practice of an organization is a small scale way to grow or shrink its own realization of its espoused mission and values.

Create a culture of celebrating the small victories. Seed trusting relationships, notice and attend to your learning, harvest your excellence.

Critique is important, but if it dominates the culture, it becomes impossible to sustain motivation and forward motion. Critique should be seen as a set of brakes—use it to help the group move at the right pace, not speed ahead of themselves, their analysis, their skill, their capacity.

Most of the time when the group feels overwhelmed by the task at hand, the task is too big. Make it smaller, find the practices that can help create the shift. It takes humility to attend to the small practices, changes and steps that actually lead to massive change. One moment of humility makes room for another.

Remember, what seems like a small step to you may not actually be small for the group. Talking about something is wildly different from undertaking it—it takes a huge effort to shift something small and fundamental. Our groups rarely have small visions. Often, a small step needs to be repeated, become a practice, in order to produce a new capacity or shape in the group, or leadership, or even in just one person. Support your groups to build up to the right size scale through practice.

Observation and Feeling

You need to be able to accurately observe and feel other humans' emotions in order to facilitate a group through a complex process.

Or be willing to ask what's happening, without your ego getting in the way of listening. Humility allows us to hear where we need to adjust, where the group needs to be held more gently or firmly.

Your sensations and emotions can be your best data in a moment of holding.

> Once upon a time I was having a hard moment with a loved one. We asked our friend Susan Raffo to hold space for us. She asked us to sit face to face and speak to each other about what was happening between us. We spoke, flowing back and forth with words, truth, tears. At a certain point we lost each other, and Susan stopped us and said, "I feel disassociation in the space. Can we slow down and find out where it is?" She had sensed that we'd lost each other, and with no assumptions about why, invited us to feel the moment, the truth, the connection. We dropped back in and found our way back to each other.

Somatics is the purest methodology I have found for learning to feel.[1] Somatics is a practice of mind/body connection that explores internal and relational physical perception and experience. Somatics teaches us to center, to find a place within ourselves that we can return to no matter what condition we're in, a place from which to make intentional choices about how we want to show up, lead, and hold.

Bodywork, yoga, and martial arts of all kinds also help. Breathing, listening, feeling for what you are capable of, noticing pain and discomfort and tingles and movement and any other feeling—all of these are part of the journey.

As facilitators, we must learn to discern when we're feeling **a** way forward, versus **the** most elegant and right next step for this particular group of people. I can often see a way forward that doesn't suit where a group actually is, the trust they actually have in this moment.

To make more possible, deepen the trust.

It's very rare to have a 100 percent emotional alignment in a room. It happens, an ecstatic moment, a grief moment. Even then, there are different degrees to which people can feel. Some will be wide open, others cracked just the smallest bit. Instead of seeking totality, you want to attend to movement and momentum. Who are the people who generate movement? Who stops it? Who critiques but never acts? Who acts but never reflects? The way forward is a river moving through these obstacles. Who pulls the bottom out, creating a waterfall which is fast, but not necessarily flowing forward? Who only thrives in the rapids? Who can't see the beauty of the riverbank because they are focused on the ocean they want to reach? The river balances all of these factors, adapting constantly to keep the right pace for the water and fish and sediment to find their ways home.

---

1. Somatics is explored in-depth in *Emergent Strategy* and *Pleasure Activism*. You can find out more about the lineage I have studied at generativesomatics.org.

Not a Missing Ingredient

You are not the missing ingredient to add diversity/fun/magic/ color to the culture of the group.[2]

This phenomenon, of being a person asked to singularly represent "otherness," happens often when facilitating dominant culture groups—wealthy people, philanthropists, majority-white groups, masculine-culture groups: You (I am mostly speaking to women of color, based on my own experience) are invited to facilitate a meeting, but in the process you are asked to sing, or to dance, or build an altar, or bring in a chant—to inject some aspect of your culture, or assumed culture, for the sake of the meeting's culture.

Your job is not to cover the gaps in the culture of the group. Your job is especially not to inject diversity into a monocultural group.

Do not be a minstrel version of yourself.

Do not perform your ethnicity or race for money.

Do not sit by and be complicit in cultural appropriation and cooptation.

When it feels like you are being asked to do so, here are some responses:

- I am really glad you are thinking about the cultural aspects of this meeting—that shows you want to invite more from the people in this group than just their labor. But it feels like you are reaching beyond the cultural reality/presence of your group to do so.
- What are the cultures present on your staff? In your network/community/board? Let's generate cultural practices for this meeting from those lineages.
- I am not comfortable with your request—it feels like you want me to perform my culture. Let's explore why you are making this request, and what needs to be learned, or done, to let this be a moment of growth.

---

2. This is different in a multiracial, multicultural space. You get to choose how much you want to weave your culture into the space. Also, dominance can show up in a lot of ways. You are still not required to bring those additional cultural offerings if it doesn't feel like an organic offer from you.

Trust As A Fractal Construct

How trustworthy are you? How do you know when to trust others? Do you know how to grow trust between yourself and others?

In facilitation, you want to be trustworthy to your group—don't over promise and under deliver, and don't pretend you understand that which you really don't.

Different levels of truth are required for different kinds of work—some groups, especially movement direct-action entities, need to be able to trust each other in life-or-death conditions. Other groups need to be able to trust each other to move resources together. Others only need enough trust for a broad coalition, light alignment to move towards a common goal.

If the trust needs to be deeper, you will need to give the group more time and space to drop in with each other. Any group that is supposed to make decisions together needs to have some basic trust-building time.

These days, it's not unusual to sit in a meeting where there is barely any actual presence—everyone is behind a computer or on their phones, sometimes participating in multiple meetings at the same moment. Some of this is a function of modern life—we have short attention spans and a multitude of distractions.

Some of this is because there is a strong need for radical movement leadership and labor, paired with a scarcity of time and resources for deep leadership development, which results in a smaller-than-necessary number of leaders holding a ton of urgent and very necessary roles.

Some of this is the ego that is born out of insecurity. By moving from point to point but barely being anywhere, we can make ourselves look and feel important, covering the truth that we often don't know what we're doing, how to contribute, or what our value is outside of constant production.

We have movements whose members struggle to trust each other at a time when those who oppose us can easily track and weaponize that distrust. It is strategic to take the time to build internal trust in our work.

Everything changes when people are face to face. I was once with author, scientist, and spiritual teacher Barbara Holmes in a Beloved Community gathering in which she explained how the heartbeat creates a 360-degree vibrational field. When we are in proximity to each other, she taught, we are literally sitting in each other's fields, co-creating a vibration unique to us.[3] As often as you reasonably can, move people into proximity with each other, into direct conversation and mutual exchange of energy.[4]

Allow relationships in the room to grow at the scale of reality—initially one to one. Then grow into family sized units, three to eight people. Ten is big, ten is a lot of people to try and find common ground within.

The scale that most movements and groups try to move in is too large for the intimacy of possibility.

Our work as facilitators is to help every group find ways to generate intimacy, deepen relationship, and learn respect for each other. Each connection between two people in the room is a thread, and as they connect, the group can weave into a fabric strong enough to hold the collective through change and crisis.

If there's no conversation possible at the level of pairs, there will be no conversation possible for the whole room.

Build the trust person to person and then let it begin to flow through the room. In a meeting where trust is required to move the content, pair people up as soon as you can after getting started— even if each person doesn't trust every single other person, after the first pairing, you'll know that each person is building trust with at least one other person. The more pairs you can create, the more pathways there will be for connection and trust in the room.

It is quite remarkable to have a room of hundreds willing to move forward together because they trust at least two other people in the space. This is what I sometimes think of as trust flocking, finding the balance between depth of connection and quantity of connections that allows the group to move in sync, on purpose, as something larger than the sum of its parts.

---

3. Facilitation science is dreamy.
4. Even in a virtual environment, pairs and small groups allow more intimacy to build.

trust the people (a spell)

lessons from the emergent strategy immersion new orleans:

trust the people who move toward you and already feel like home.

trust the people to let you rest.

trust the people to do everything better than you could have imagined.

trust the people and they become trustworthy.

trust that the people are doing their work to trust themselves.

trust that each breach of trust can deepen trust or clarify boundaries.

trust the people who revel in pleasure after hard work.

trust the people who let children teach/remind us how to emote, be still, and laugh.

trust the people who see and hold your heart.

trust the people who listen to the whales.

trust the people and you will become trustworthy.

trust the people and show them your love.

trust the people.

Practices For Fractal Facilitation

Practice observation when you're in any room. Make notes to yourself when the energy shifts, when the collective mood changes, even (especially) when the changes are small.

Make sure there are plenty of small ways people can support holding the container—and by container I mean both the physical space of the gathering and the logistical, documentation, and energetic needs of the group. Tasks that can be distributed include taking and/or compiling notes both digital and butcher paper, summarizing the day, facilitating small groups, facilitating icebreakers and stretches, documenting historic moments with photography, social media posting (if the group has agreed to such documentation and it suits the security culture).[5]

---

5. See more about security culture in "We Keep Us Safe: Facilitating Safer Spaces" by Ejeris Dixon starting on page 83 in the Black Feminist Wisdom section.

Align the container with the values, so that there are lots of places to practice being liberated together. The values of a group, what they care about and want to generate in the world, are one of the first things they can and should articulate with each other. The values can continue to be revisited as the group learns what they care about based on where they put their time, attention, and other resources. Everything from how you provide water and food, to the gender access of bathrooms, to the way the group introduces themselves can help to align the group with the world they are working to create. Values don't mean much if there is no way to put them into practice and action. Wherever there is time and capacity, attend to these fractal ways that the container you are in represents the world you are generating.

Notice and celebrate every small step towards the vision/goal/ objective/dream/intention. Every step. If there is only forward motion without noticing and celebration, the group will get exhausted and have no sense that they are making the incremental changes that eventually build into monumental change. Notice, and invite everyone in the group to pay attention to and celebrate their collective work.

Grow rigor with small, repeated practices, and invite people to practice in relationship. For most participants in our current political moment, rigor is less compelling than relationship and the projection of expertise. Practice is the path to embodiment, which is when a way of being is not just something we believe in our minds, but something our bodies can fully hold, something that becomes a default in our behaviors, choices, and actions.

We embody whatever society shaped us to be and believe until we awaken to the reality that we can change, we can shape ourselves, we are constantly changing, and we can reorient ourselves to grow towards life that is collective and collaborative. In the same way that repetition of a practice is the path to embodiment for an individual, being in collective practice is the path to embodiment in a group.[6] Practice rigor together—collectivize being on

---

6. According to Richard Strozzi-Heckler, three hundred repetitions lead to muscle memory, three thousand lead to embodiment. See strozziinstitute.com.

time for shared work, collectivize holding a sacred space, collectivize non-dramatic accountability, collectivize creating a container of transformation.

Create moments of doing the right thing. Doing the right thing is less compelling for many people than being seen/assumed to be doing the right thing.[7] As a facilitator, you have to see the trauma in a collective shape, the pain that leads to procrastination, the hopelessness and heartache that yield pontification, the exhaustion and apathy of shady behavior. Slice thru, start small, create a moment of doing the right thing. Let people get a felt sense for being on the right side of history. Let that alignment galvanize and deepen political commitment for the next steps.

---

7.   I blame organized religion—putting the performance before the substance.

Fractal Mediation

Mediation is a fractal art. Helping two people, or a small group, resolve conflict in ways that don't involve violence, prison, the police,
or public shaming, is crucial for our species learning to practice
justice at a collective level. It's fundamentally about noticing small
things—a flicker of emotion can be the first small step towards big
accountability. Below are some best practices for the fractal aspects
of mediation.

Understand that mediation generally breaks down into smaller
phases. In some cases, these phases can all happen in one session;
in other cases, the phases happen over time. Here's how I define
the phases:[1]

- **Surrender:** The initial phase of acknowledging that mediation is needed and why.
- **Landscape:** Both/all parties laying out the landscape of
  tension/conflict as they see/feel it. This can happen by
  email or phone call, but I recommend it is done one-on-
  one with the mediator.
- **Listening:** This is the heart of the mediation—as the mediator you are holding a wide space to allow the mediated
  parties to hear each other. A very rudimentary tool here is
  to have people reflect back to each other *what* they hear,
  and *that* they are hearing each other.

---

1. See Kitchen Table Mediation in the "Transformative Justice / Resilience Mediation" chapter for more details on running a mediation.

- **Negotiation:** Here we identify what both/all parties need in order to move forward. Apologies? Boundaries? New behavior? Closure? A new narrative to your community?
  - As the mediator you are listening for these needs and requests throughout, and particularly paying attention to where the requests might be at odds. For example, if one person wants to be in better communication and the other needs to not speak again for the foreseeable future, your job as the mediator is to hold up the reality, the gap between the needs, and help them land in a solution that affirms the different desires. Help them see what is and is not possible at this time. Usually the person in need of boundaries or closure takes precedent, as no one can be required to stay in a relationship for any reason.
- **Closure:** The closing of the mediation should be clean as a whistle. Very clearly stating the next steps, boundaries, agreements, and if there is anything else expected of either party.
  - In some cases, I will instruct participants to communicate through a third party (very, very rarely is that third party me) for the foreseeable future, while the mediation is ongoing, or for a set period of time upon completion of the mediation. This is particularly useful for a mediation of people who are in common movement locations and need to end their personal relationship. This phase of mediation can be the most dangerous phase for the community, because the impulse to publicly destroy each other is high and the means are readily available.

Pay attention to what both/all parties are needing. One of the most helpful things we can do as mediators is to help people clearly articulate what they need in order to experience closure, clarify boundaries, or regenerate a positive relationship. So many of us think we are communicating clearly when we are speaking through clouds in a wildly circuitous manner. As the mediator you can keep trimming off the hyperbole and looping so that the participants can hear the essence of the conflict.

Plan the mediation in bite-size chunks.

- I often aim for an hour at a time. I want to ensure that the conversation stays focused, and that there is enough emotional energy for covering the necessary work.

- If a conversation has no container, one or more of the people who need help can end up completely emotionally exhausted. Especially limit the time if you suspect there are harmful dynamics afoot in the situation—imbalanced power or emotional labor.

- Particularly if you have people who can get lost in long monologues, repeating stories, infinite loops of blame, you can focus them by letting them in on what the end time is. In extreme cases I have set a timer that allows people to have a sense of when the time is winding down. When people struggle in conflict they can lose touch with how much time they are spending in the reliving phase of mediation.

- Celebrate the work you are able to do.

- Seek moments of clear request, clear offer, clear accountability/apology. Highlight and slow down these moments.

Finally, you can ask people some hopeful questions:

- That sounded like a request/offer/apology. Can you say it one more time?

- Can you respond to that request/offer?

- Can you clarify what you are apologizing for?

- Can you take in that accountability/apology?

Intentional Adaptation Facilitation

Brief Thoughts on Intentional Adaptation

Change is constant. You can't stop change, control change, or perfectly plan change. You can ride the waves of change, partner with change, and shape change.

Adaptation is long term or structural change in a creature or system to account for a need for survival. Adaptation is not about being reactionary, changing without intention, or being victimized, controlled, and tossed around by the inevitable changes of life. It's about shaping change and letting changes make us stronger as individual and collective bodies.

How do we get relaxed and intentional in the face of change?

Get curious, in your own life, about how you face change in powerful ways, in ways that show your dignity and help you stay connected to what you care about. The more you practice this in yourself, the more you will be able to embody and support dignified change in the groups you hold.

Think of the tenderness with which you hold a newborn. Everything is connected, resilient, and growing, and you have the control, the strength, the power to actually protect the small and new from the chaotic world.

Think of holding a child's hand at a crossroads. Yes, now they can run around for themselves and hold up their head and tell you they promise to look both ways, but sometimes you still see the danger they don't see and you pull them into you, scoop them up, hold them close as they perhaps still try to move towards fun/harm.

Think of holding an elder, supporting her up out of her bed and into a chair, so you can change the sheets. Her body is fragile, slow, deteriorating. Her mind wanders but she also still knows exactly what she wants. To hold her is to guide without directing, to catch the weight she didn't expect to throw her off balance, to protect her dignity while attending to her care.

Care. Attention. This is the way to practice intentional adaptation in facilitation.

Adaptation is a way our systems make sense of all that we're feeling.

Loving life means committing to the adaptation to stay alive, rather than the stubbornness to stay the same.

Adaptations are guided by what we can feel, in ourselves and in relationship to others. Birds murmurate through the sky according to no schematic—they feel each other and shift together. If plans aren't informed by feelings, they will inevitably end up inhumane, out of right relationship with the planet.

Our feelings, when we attend to them, ARE our nature, guiding us to evolve, grow, break fatal habits, generate health and healing. Feelings are not the truth, but can often face you in the right direction, pointed toward the truth. When you are facilitating a group, the strong feelings are indications that adaptations are needed—a slowing down, a pairing or small-group moment, a deepening into values alignment, a fine tuning of vision.

Acknowledging big feelings, particularly fear, can open us up to understand feelings as data and take appropriate action.

Intentions / Longings

There are so many ways to articulate what you long for. Vision, dream, longing, commitment, goal, objective, idea. For some groups, what they long for comes out in the form of a shared visual, a map, a plan, a mission, a theory of change, a set of values, or principles.

In my work with Allied Media Projects, the intentions were laid out as principles that guide our collective practices. Those principles show up throughout these pages, they are so fundamental to my worldview: we begin by listening; we presume our power not our powerlessness; wherever there is a problem, there are already people working on the solution; center and follow the innovative solutions that come from those living in intersecting crises, because those solutions work in the widest range of conditions.

In my work with generative somatics, we learned to make declarations, or commitments: statements that speak to who we are becoming in service of the world we are working to create. We speak our commitments in the pattern of "I am a commitment to," so that each time we say our commitment we are declaring ourselves an embodiment of our longings. As I write this book, I am a commitment to resilient movements that sustain and deepen under the pressures of change and difference. I am a commitment to trusting love the way I trust gravity. I am a decade along my student path in somatics, and over the years I have been a commitment to telling my story in order to love my whole self, to authentic intimacy and generative boundaries, to leading from my deep oceanic center, and to deep satisfaction, ease, and intactness in every relationship. If you see these things in me, it is not an accident. And, I am still learning.

I have also been a part of many teaching teams with generative somatics where we made a team, or collective, commitment: We are a commitment to delivering a compelling, embodied experience of somatics to those on the front lines of social and environmental justice work.

Collectively, we have to know how to articulate enough to compel ourselves forward, but leave our longings open enough to invite others to join us. We have to break out of patterns of articulating destinations, and dreaming in terms of outcomes. The horizon we can see is not the end of the journey, it's just the outer limit of our vision.

Help people set intentions for how they want to be, how their children's children will feel, what the relationships will look like, how power will be shared, how governance will work, how justice will play out.

This may be controversial, but I actually think it's ok for a group to move without clearly articulated intentions for a little while, to move based on feeling the unspoken, perhaps unspeakable, pattern. It's ok to be drawn towards each other, drawn into connection and motion. It's ok to take some actions, learn how and who each other are. Pay attention to what the group chooses to do and how they do it. I used to always start with vision, but with reflection I've seen that the intentions, vision, and values can sometimes emerge more clearly inside the work and relationships. Longings are intimate. They shouldn't be thrown at each other as gauntlets, tests, or escalators we have to keep moving up in order to earn our place in the group.

That said, in order to grow, in order to have impact, people do eventually need to articulate what they long for. As a facilitator, you need to make sure, above all else, that the deepest longings within the group align.

Our intentions and longings should be the center of our lives and our work. Our collective intentions and longings should be the center of our movements.

Questions to help people unveil their collective longings, and to help you articulate your own facilitation commitment:

- What do we most want for our species?
- What do we most want for our children's children?
- How do we want it to feel in the space between us?
- How do we know where we belong, and who we belong to?
- What is the texture/scent/pressure/poetry of our safety?
- What is my/our legacy?
- When do we get to just be?

Values-Based Logistics

Your intentions, values, and beliefs should inform the logistics of the space. Any meeting or gathering is a place to practice the future together in the most tangible ways. Logistics are one of the ways to intentionally adapt our collective behaviors together! Consider questions such as:

- What kinds of humans do we want to be and become?
- In what kind of culture, and society, do those humans thrive?
- What kind of structures and practices do we need to be in to generate that future?

The adaptations you make in the space should be rooted in what you care about. Some common logistical practices that are relevant in the political moment of this book:

- We are in a climate catastrophe. Meetings shouldn't use plastic water bottles, Styrofoam plates, unnecessary fuel, or require unnecessary travel.
- Food is one of the ways we practice community together. Feed people justice food, food that is local, organic, sourced from known entities, food that has stories, food that the growers and cooks are excited to share.
- Bathrooms are a great place to practice a gender-liberated present and make it our norm. Negotiation of the bathroom space is a way to educate the building management in places that still hold a bathroom-binary culture, and to educate participants with an immediate opportunity to practice.
- Access needs: Pre-survey your group to assess the needs for transportation shuttles, wheelchair-accessible meeting spaces, elevators for multi-floor spaces, and translators for multilingual spaces (including sign language). For virtual meetings, plan for sustainable amounts of screen time, chat options, food delivery coupons—these are just a few ways to practice creating a space in which the maximum number of participants can feel the belonging needed to co-create.

- Shift how you think about waste. Extra materials should be donated to local organizers in need. Extra food should go to those who are hungry. Recycle as much as possible. Compete to have as little landfill as possible at the end of your gatherings.

  Every facilitation container you create is a microcosm of your beliefs. What future are you committed to?

Intentional Adaptation Agendas

Build agendas that can breathe and pivot.

Most conversations take a minimum of an hour to move well, and decision-making conversations can take longer, may need breaks or days between them. If you look at, or are asked to produce, an agenda where meaningful conversations are being given thirty minutes or less, be wary. Negotiate with the group to give priority conversations more time. If the group is stubborn around overdoing it, find out the top priorities of the meeting and place those earlier in the time so there's less risk of getting cut off from the most important work.

An agenda can feel rigid and scarce in terms of time and attention, or it can feel spacious, lush, emergent. The difference is determined by the conversations that happen beforehand, identifying the right focus and priorities, the trust people have in each other and in the facilitator, and the culture that is set around time. I have traveled a lot, and it took me a while to come to see, understand, and respect the truth that most of our work is not as urgent as racialized capitalism makes it look. The groups I facilitate often have a toxic relationship to time, seeing everything as urgent in a scarce container. I am committed to holding an abundant relationship to time, which means I don't contribute to a scarce time narrative unless conditions are dire (a weather crisis is unfolding, for example, or a deportation attempt is going to happen and direct action is needed).

Here's my basic meeting agenda template, which I often create in Excel so I can easily drag things about to change and rearrange events based on feedback, or shifting times in the room, and not lose detail:

Date/Time	Agenda	Details	Who/How[1]
4/20/42 10-10:30am	Land Acknowledgment and Welcome	Local tribe leadership honored and asked permission to do this work. Welcome participants to the meeting and give basic logistics and access information	Name Tables and supplies set up Mic set up
10:30am	Agenda Review	Review agenda and make sure that people see it will meet their exectations and needs	Facilitator A (name)
10:45am	Agreements	Revisit agreements for how we will hold space with each other, see if any additions are needed	Facilitator B (name)
11:00am	Opening Discussion	How have we done as an organization since the last time we were gathered? Are we proud of our work? What have we learned?	Facilitator A Small groups, harvest

1. For a meeting of over ten people, I may add a separate column for How/Supplies.

And here is my basic agenda flow:

Welcome/Grounding Help everyone arrive in ways that honor the culture of your group, the place you're in, and the kind of meeting you're having.

Check-ins In small, familiar groups have everyone say how they are, what those working with them today should be aware of, maybe answer a check-in question to deepen the collective relationship. In groups that don't know each other well, do check-ins in pairs; in large groups, do check-ins in pairs and then ask for some sharing of the range. Let people know that however they are doing and feeling, they're welcome.

Updates (customize)

- Existing work, including updates from the to-do list from last meeting if relevant
- Finances
- Schedules

Discussions

- Exploratory (guiding questions include "What do y'all think of this?" "What should be included in a proposal about this?" "Are we interested in doing this?'), 15–20 minute discussions
- Planning (guiding questions include "What's the Timeline?" "Who's doing each task?" "Does this still align with our values/capacity/strategy?" "What are the conditions of satisfaction—how will we know we have completed this in a satisfactory way?") 30–60 minute discussions
- Decision making (I favor proposal-based consensus! Make decisions based on proposals, so that your moves are based on good data and answered questions. If possible, work towards consensus, and do work as a group that everyone is excited about.) 30–90 minute discussions

Take breaks every ninety minutes or so (set the timing based on the culture of your group. Some groups need more breaks due to shifts in attention span or bodily comfort needs, even if it's just a bio break for water to go in and out of the body. Encourage stretching and movement.

Review Next Steps

Close with appreciation

For a multi-day meeting, open with welcome and grounding each day, close with appreciation, and arrange the discussions to allow for breaks.

If you want to have a more emergent agenda, create a list of possible discussions (you can do this with a pre-survey, or post-its/index cards/recycled paper on site) and work together to select which conversations happen during each discussion window.

In large groups, you can hold multiple conversations simultaneously, as long as you have a solid harvest (timed, structured report back) at the end where the key lessons and/or decisions from the conversations come back to the whole group.

The more trust your group develops, the easier it is to play with emergent agenda development. For the Emergent Strategy Ideation Institute collective, we stagger facilitation such that, for our weekly staff meetings, a different person holds the agenda and moves us through it each time. Between meetings we all have access to a running agenda document and can add items for the upcoming meeting. At the top of the meeting, the facilitator for that session makes sure we've articulated everything that needs to be covered in our ninety minutes together, and which things are top priority. Then we answer a check-in question and move through the items with a lot of ease and laughter. We trust each other, and trust each person to do the work of their role, so we trust that people will give each other the necessary updates, won't waste time belaboring things that either aren't ready for decision or aren't worth the attention of the whole group, and we trust our communal prioritization.

It can take a while to pivot from a culture of rigid time-scarce agendas to lush spacious adaptive agendas, but it is worth the clunky learning phase for organizations that are in regular meetings with each other. With practice, you become a flock, moving together through content, time, space, and strategy as bodies and minds trusting the connections with each other.

Practices for Intentional Adaptation

To raise your awareness of intentional (and unintentional) adaptation, ask to **attend meetings as an observer**. Track every shift you see happen during a meeting. Make notes—was the change a reaction? An adaptation? Does it move the group towards their intentions or throw them off course? Notice (without judgment, with curiosity) when you would make different choices than the facilitator of the room. Watch how it plays out, activate your imagination, learn.

When the room feels unclear, **shift your location** in the meeting space. Change your perspective, don't take your position for granted.

Ask the room to **suggest one change** they think would shift the future of the organization, campaign, gathering.

Practice getting still…though, this is not precise. Stillness is not something we *get,* but more of an existing state we return to. It is much easier to feel an adaptation from a still, centered place. In the room, what I mean is: get more connected. Quiet, tune in to all the life around you.

Centering. One of the most important practices of intentional adaptation I have ever learned is the centering practice[2] which is core to somatics, and traces its roots back to aikido, tai chi, and other martial arts.

Below is an extended centering practice:[3]

Sitting, standing, or laying down, notice what *is* without judgment, or trying to fix yourself. Notice things like temperature, tension, pain, activity, your clothing on your skin, your mood, your pace. Even notice where you might be numb, and how deeply you can breathe. It might take a few moments to scan your body and notice all the sensations, emotions, moods.

Now you are going to center on purpose. Bring your attention to the center of your being, which on many human bodies is

---

2. I first learned this practice from Spenta Kandawalla as a student of generative somatics. Staci Haines, Alta Starr, Denise Perry, Nathan Shara, Mawulisa Thomas-Adeyemo, Jennifer Ianello, Jennifer Toles, Nazbah Tom, and many others shaped the practice I most consistently work with.
3. You can find a beautiful version of the practice online, guided by Prentis Hemphill.

about two inches below the belly button, the midpoint between the soles of our feet and the tops of our skulls. It can help to place your hand on your lower belly/pelvic bowl to feel your center in your palm, and let the sensation of your hand bring your attention to center. Sometimes, you can bring a hand or ask someone to touch your back at your sacrum, so you can feel the 360 degrees of your center. If your eyes have closed, or you have otherwise turned inwards, you're invited to re-open them and stay in connection for the centering practice—we want to learn to center while in touch with the world.

From this center, fill into length. Feel the sensations of length along the body, and, without effort, relax into your full length, your full dignity. This may mean giving more of ourselves to gravity, feeling an extension into relationship with the earth. If you are sitting or standing, it may mean imagining a string gently inviting your head up to the stars. Raise and drop your shoulders. The dignity you are centering is organic, it's yours, it isn't a performance or a puffing up. One of the things trauma can steal away from us is dignity—so many methods of oppression have led to a shrinking, looking down, hunkering in. Each time we center in our full length and dignity, we are reclaiming our original selves. Center in dignity.

From that dignity, we center in width. Imagine a scroll unfurling from your spine to the outer edges of your being. Feel the sensations of width as your lungs fill with air. Notice if you favor one side or the other in your hips. Feel the boundaries along the outer edges of yourself—where do you end? Where does the person next to you begin? Feel your boundaries, let them be solid and porous. Width as a dimension is where we practice taking up space, where we assert that we all have the right to take up space. This is also the horizontal dimension of connection, of the collective, of being in circle with others. We have the right to be in right relationship with others, connected, with healthy boundaries.

In our dignity and spacious, balanced connection, we center in our depth. Within, this means giving more depth—stop sucking in your gut or your butt, relax, feel the depth from the front of your heart to the back of it, the front of your stomach to the back. You are three dimensional.

Now, feel the sensations on the back of your body—maybe the texture of a shirt, or wind across your shoulders. At our backs is our history, lineage, all that came before this moment, both in our own lives and in the long journey of our species, our societies, our landscapes, our planet, our universe. So much has conspired to bring about this particular moment. You may even feel the presence of known and unknown ancestors at your back.

Coming through the body, balance between what's behind and what's ahead. At our fronts you can also feel the sensations of wind, clothing. Sometimes I notice the feeling of my breath on my upper lip as it leaves my body. Out ahead of us lies the unknown, the mystery—that which we will shape together. Feel the depth of your lifetime, and this moment. Center in your depth.

What is it you love, what is it you most long for? Whatever vision you have of the future, who is it you must be in order to realize that vision? Feel that love and longing in the center of your being and let it fill you up with purpose. If you have a commitment, speak it to yourself now.

Notice your mood. If you are centering with others, share that mood in a word or two. Mood is not the state of your body, but your emotional state.

Here are a couple of shorter centering practices:
Center:
Bring your attention to center.
Feel your dignity, your right to take up space, your

connection with others, and your relationship with the arc of your life.

What is your purpose? Let that fill you up.

What is your mood?

Breath:

Let your breath guide you into your body, into your center.

Let your length be long.

Let your width be wide.

Let your depth be deep.

Feel yourself on purpose.

Centering Song:

Long as the light

Wide as the sea

Deep as the dirt

I'm gonna be me

I'm gonna be free

Intentional Adaptation Mediation

Mediation is an intentional move to change the conditions or dynamics of a relationship. In many situations, it is a move from reactive and chaotic, dysfunctional conflict into intentional and potentially generative conflict.

You want to understand the intentions of the people you are mediating, and help them make the right changes together.

Here are some best practices you can use:

As the mediator, have a clear sense of what both/all parties want from the session(s). This usually entails either having individual conversations beforehand, or asking for a private email explaining what is going on, what the issue is, and what they need in order to move forward. This kind of reflection can help people move from general complaint and/or anger into a stance of intentions, needs, demands. As the mediator, part of how you can help the conversation move forward is to let them know where their longings are aligned, and where they are at odds.

Ignore the tangents, follow the feelings. Sometimes tangents move on the path of feeling, but not always, not often. Often they are looping around the feeling—spiraling up or down from the feeling.

Ask hopeful questions like, "How does that connect to what you need in this moment?" or suggest that they take a breath and ask, "What is the essence of the point you are trying to make right now?"

People and conditions change! That's a universal constant. But that doesn't mean this dynamic will evolve, or will change soon enough to matter for these people. Acknowledge that change is constant and still give your pair/group permission for boundaries, or quitting the dynamic.

Keep reminding the participants that change is possible. Explain that by being in this conversation in good faith, they are making something else possible. At the same time, let them know that it is possible to quit the aspects of the dynamic that don't work. That it is possible to have a connection that suits both/all of their needs.

Be attentive to when they might need a different process. Some adaptations include:

- Breaking the mediation into shorter sessions, focused around specific aspects of conflict.
- Have more than one mediator so that each person has someone to hold space specifically for their needs.
- Escalate to a community accountability process if what is unveiled in the mediation is in the realm of physical, emotional, financial, or verbal abuse/manipulation/gaslighting.
- Change the location/setting—go outside, move to a different room, open a window, stretch break, shift locations around the table.

Nonlinear/Iterative Facilitation

Brief Thoughts on Nonlinear/Iterative Facilitation

A lifetime is miraculous and brief—don't waste it! Celebrate every beautiful, tiny thing you can notice or learn.

Time is one of the least understood aspects of our collective experience.

We are born, we age, we die, as individuals, collectives, groups, generations, eras, nations. We are cared for, then we care for others, then we are cared for again. There is a linear aspect to our experiences that can make us think that age or years will result in certain wisdoms or expertise.

But what matters more than that linear path is what we are repeating and upgrading in cycles inside of our time. We are always practicing something, and those practices move us towards and away from liberation. The relationship we have to time is also a practice. If we pay attention, we can shift the relationship we have with time from scarcity to abundance, from obligatory to desired, from a policed, colonized space to a practice ground on which to learn to live liberated lives.

Change moves in the same nonlinear way a love story moves. Towards, away, up, down, close, far, growing, always growing. When we are creating community efforts we grow towards each other and then away, we root into community, we reach for impact, sometimes we outgrow each other, or we grow into new formations.

We learn through an accumulation of lessons. We change through an accumulation of practices.

Accumulation is a crucial part of nonlinear change—letting depth and practice accumulate in your collective system. Octavia Butler teaches, "Belief initiates and guides action, or it does nothing." It's not about how many times you say you'll change, it's about accumulating the benefits of practicing changes in your system.

Release perfection.[1] The idea of iteration is that we are repeating—not failing, but practicing and learning. And with each repetition there are things to learn, notice, grow from. Love the body that does the practice, love the imbalance that yields to balance, love the shaking muscles that grow strong, love the fumbling tongue that becomes fluent, love the chaos that finds an organic and exciting center. Let love show up and change the possibilities.

Learning From Your Mistakes

Mistakes, or what feel like mistakes, can be a way of learning the culture of the group, helping them see themselves. Something that initially feels like a mistake can be a learning opportunity— what makes this group tender? Angry? Freeze? What enlivens this group into action? What makes them rush into wasteful action? Do they take responsibility, cast blame, become victims of their own decisions? Hurry to fix the narrative, or claim the reality? Do mistakes deepen their trust, or decimate it?

Learn to examine your individual and collective mistakes. Learn from your decisions and actions in order to understand where you can pivot, grow, adapt, or close an experiment. This is what turns a failure into a lesson.

Learn to acknowledge when what is happening is not what you planned to happen. As the facilitator, it is particularly important to be able to take accountability if things are not going to hit the

---

1. "Perfection is a commitment to habitual self-doubt." —Prentis Hemphill.

articulated goal. You may get to a place more necessary, but do so without hiding the shift in direction.

Learn to take responsibility when something you planned, or a space that you created or held, caused harm, intentionally or, much more often, not.

Don't lie. If the group is off course, say so. Let them be mindful in their mistakes, to see their choices with dignity.

Encourage experimentation! Help the group to relinquish the paths of familiar failure, which are often acceptable to philanthropy.[2]

To get better results, to even imagine a true victory (a win that elevates our basic rights and needs out of the space of political debate), we must experiment with different strategies and tactics, different formations.

The experimental is uncomfortable, it shifts the conversation from "why didn't someone do X?" to "how will we do X in alignment with our values?" or "what can we co-create?"

Experiments are how we practice our "power with," instead of over, each other.

Lineage

Most of us learn to facilitate as part of a larger calling to heal, bring wholeness, listen, support. I think that being in a space that is well facilitated can be healing, feel healing.

We need facilitation that accounts for groups and facilitators with multiple lineages and cultural contexts. If one particular mode of facilitation speaks to you (visioning, conflict resolution, strategic development, organizational development, annual planning, etc),

---

2.   I have a longstanding critique of philanthropy, where the money is coming from and often controlled by privileged people who are not necessarily invested in changing conditions, but are donating for a tax write-off. Philanthropy asks for unreasonable amounts of labor from movements, both to access and account for resources, and for the continuous demand to show measurables in processes that are only given months for experimentation. It's a set-up for perpetual failure or working towards results that still uphold unjust power dynamics. I have written and offered training to funders interested in applying emergent strategy to their work, which in the long run is fundamentally a path decolonizing and redistributing their resources.

follow that path. It's ok to specialize and prioritize. It's useful to movements if we deepen into excellence in the areas we choose to work.

Many of us have multiple lineages, including multiple economic locations, racial and ethnic inheritances, movement teachers, concurrent careers, and spiritual paths that our ancestors have embodied. Our best work together comes at intersections and in combinations of those lineages.

Octavia said, "embrace diversity!" Many of us in movement have been intentionally cut off from our healing power, our legacies of right relationship. In the rooms where we hold change, we have to drop the assumption of shared cultural or spiritual practices in order to feel for the right practices for the whole group, the combination of practices that perhaps can only flow through us. Release the myth of monoculture.

"I am a commitment to teaching in my own tongue," Prentis Hemphill tells us. What does it look like to make room for many lineages to be present and guide the space, for many tongues to be spoken and deeply understood?

Practices for Nonlinear/Iterative Facilitation

Find the next relevant conversation. Don't be afraid to depart from the agenda if another conversational need becomes crystal clear.

Generate agendas together. In small, intimate groups (two, four), have brief conversations on what is important for this gathering. Give each small group a couple of small post-it notes to write, clearly, what they most want the group to spend our time on. In the large group, synthesize the suggestions, clustering the ones that are aligned into columns or stars. If it's a lot of conversations, have the group prioritize them. Let the priorities set your collective direction.

Best case scenario, **have a break every ninety minutes** to allow biological needs to be met. Stretch often; encourage movement, stepping outside, and hydration. Invite play. All of the space and breaks built into the agenda are time for reflection, thoughtfulness, and re-energizing the bodies carrying the thoughts.

When you get stuck, **ask the people** in the room what needs to be discussed by them at this time. If the group is large or in tension, ask them to write it down on scraps of paper and then send them on a break so you can synthesize their feedback.

Map change processes.
- Map your own love stories, how you have learned to love.
- Map how you ended up where you are.
- Map your political development.
- Map how change actually happens in your life.
- . Learn to respect the non-linear nature of change.

Make a comprehensive list of what you are currently practicing.
- Bonus: make two lists—practices that move you towards your vision for justice and liberation, and a list of practices that move you away from your vision.

Observation: when you are facilitating, **track what the group is practicing**. Be honest with yourself about what you see. What are they practicing when it comes to decision making? Justice? Sharing power? Relationship building? Decentralization?

If it's appropriate, offer a reflection. Are the group's practices in alignment with their vision?

Nonlinear/Iterative Mediation

Sometimes mediation happens in a very intentional way, with preparation, clear needs, in my/your kitchen, over tea, with clear energy and abundant time. For guidelines on that process, check out the Transformative Justice/Resilient Mediation chapter for the Kitchen Table model.

Sometimes, though, you're in a meeting and an honest moment unfolds that is bigger than what the room can hold, and your job as a mediator is to create the best conditions you can:

- Private, quiet, natural or soft light.
- Have a comfortable seating arrangement where everyone can see each other and you can easily turn people towards each other to face something together.
- Set a timer that everyone can hear to indicate 10 minutes are left, or have a clock where people can see it.

Mediation can feel very nonlinear, because what you're trying to get to is the root system of the disagreement. Our memories are not linear, they are gnarly, emotional, and biased; we can get quite committed to, sometimes tangled up in, a storyline that makes us right and the other person wrong.[1] Even as people are attempting to tell you the truth of what has unfolded between them, you as a mediator have to be listening for where there are

---

1. I highly recommend the Ted Chiang novella *Story of Your Life* on this topic.

gaps, where there's heat, where there are blocks in their ability to hear each other.

Ask what people need. Keep asking them. As truth gets told, new needs get unveiled, along with the roots of unspoken needs. Things will change and develop. Let them. Adjust your internal understanding of what will satisfy the conversation as new possibilities appear.

Eventually, every process winds down. Feel for completion. Not perfection, but the moment when the people sitting across from each other have done enough work. Sometimes this looks like a quieting, slowing down of speech. Sometimes it looks like one person getting more and more emotional while the other shuts down and withdraws—they are splitting emotionally and heading in different directions. Sometimes it looks like laughter, or even an exhale of contentment. Inside of you, you may feel a release of tension in your own gut or shoulders. I often feel a continuous tremor in my gut when there is tension in a room, and a calm opening within me when we have moved through it. Trust that feeling.

If people go (or get pushed) beyond their physical or emotional capacity, they will not be able to find satisfaction in the mediation.

Ask people what they have learned about themselves, about the other, about the relationship, the possibilities, the boundaries, and what's needed. The reflection helps you assess what's actually landing with each person.

Finally, ask the participants what one practice they choose to be in after this session. No contact? Boundaried interactions? Careful reconnection? They are moving out of the practice, the iterations, of the conflict. A clear practice to carry forward helps to solidify the new state, the post-mediated state, of the connection.

Interdependent/Decentralized Facilitation

Brief Thoughts on Interdependence and Decentralization

Interdependence is about relationships—letting your needs show appropriately, supporting others in meeting their needs.

Each life is an opportunity to realize and practice divinity, or connectedness. This is why spiritual experiences often feel like "all is one" or "we are all connected." Any meeting, gathering, or process you are holding is an opportunity to create a container for that connectedness.

Interdependence thrives when you, as a facilitator, help make the distinction between authenticity and intimacy and help participants gauge which is appropriate for the trust levels in the room. Authenticity is having integrity between what you say and how you are or what you do. Intimacy is the closeness present when you can be yourself, be honest about your needs, and share the layers and details of what you are feeling and why you behave the way you do, particularly when you feel mistaken, hurt, or not in control.

When a group is practicing inappropriate intimacy— over-sharing, no boundaries, thinking of themselves as family vs. comrades—it can lead to codependent movement spaces: work doesn't happen, or happens too slowly for impact; accountability scares people, any changing condition can take the center from the group, and so on.

Conversely, when a group shares nothing about their personal lives at all, it is very difficult to break patterns of independence, isolation, martyrdom, and burn out. It's also very difficult to generate authentic connections, because people are intentionally trying to repress their truth... Let's not require people to be inauthentic as a path into the work.

Interdependence and decentralization are present in the room when the care is mutual, vision is held by each person, and people can speak their needs and be supported in having them met.

*
* *

"Three people are better than no people."
—Fannie Lou Hamer

The people are always right.

More accurately, the people are always true to themselves. In most circumstances, they will stay true to what they believe is possible, what they understand their needs to be, and what they think their capacity is. This is an area where actions speak louder than words—track the work people actually do, the ways they communicate, the deadlines they meet, the way they distribute their financial and labor resources. The work will tell the truth of what the people care about and long for.

Your work as a facilitator is to help them see any unhelpful patterns of isolation, independence, or competition in their behavior, and let a new truth of mutual support emerge.

The people are almost never right the first time around. And they will never find their way if they don't have adequate room for both making mistakes and giving/receiving feedback.

That said, only facilitate groups you trust to make the right moves, including the right mistakes.

We are in an arc towards justice that stretches beyond our lifetimes and imaginations. We must maintain that impossible, massive vision in every room we hold.

Under pressure, people both give less room for mistakes and are much more likely to make mistakes, to overlook crucial information and dynamics. Your work is to help groups stay centered, connected, and focused under pressure, and to remove false urgency from the work.

To truly succeed, the people should define who they mean when they speak of "we," of "them," of "movement," of "the people." Ask: who are your people? Who are you accountable to? Both generally (for example, Black people) and specifically (for example, Black Organizing for Leadership and Dignity).

Preparing an agenda is the work of designing a space for an authentic engagement in content. Too often, planning bodies try to pre-process every conversation beforehand[1] and drive the group to a particular destination, sometimes because the work is being rushed, and sometimes because those in leadership don't trust the group. As a facilitator, if you are asked to hold space in this way, resist! Make room for the people coming to the gathering to contribute. Make room for the planning body to learn to trust their own people. Being together shouldn't be a performance of process. Build agendas that have room for real people to have real conversations.

If there are pieces of work that are urgent, then design decision-making processes that allow for a rapid response protocol. Don't fake a collective process for the sake of meeting an urgent deadline, this practice will eventually deteriorate trust in the group.

Trust the people by asking real questions, good questions that everyone doesn't already know the answer to. Trust the people to learn together, in real time, in small groups. Help people find each other in the space.

Serving the whole is not just catering to the majority. The majority can be engaged in harmful behaviors, and serving the whole can mean intervening on harm. Sometimes a group is moving along a path towards a compromise of their values, or an unnecessary conflict, simply because they've fallen into a pattern of groupthink. As the facilitator, your work includes being able to hold up a mirror in those moments, to ask a question that can slow things

---

1. I call this "penguin daddy" behavior.

down and make sure the group is in their intentions—"Just checking, is this aligned with your values?"

Sometimes you need to break the room into smaller units organized by identity, class, or other unique experiences that will remind them that they are showing up in the room not just for individual purposes, but as an act of accountability to larger bodies and communities.

Facilitators are also people, often people who wrestle with belonging, loneliness, imposter syndrome, martyrdom, just like anyone else. Have your own support circle where you can let your needs show, grow community to hold you as you hold others.

Decentralization is the biggest lesson of the Black civil rights movement in the US—isolated, rock-star leaders are vulnerable. Movements that put all of their eggs in one leader's basket are vulnerable movements. Decentralizing vision, strategy, and work creates resilient movements.

Decentralized and interdependent movements are not without hierarchy. There can be healthy organic hierarchies of experience, skill expertise, or areas of focus. I, for instance, am down to surrender to the leadership of others on budgets, and down to take more leadership in the work of resolving harm or generating vision.

Attending to Trust and Presence

"Strong people don't need strong leaders."
—Ella Baker

Trust gets built one to one.

Trust is built and strengthened in small ways…don't wait until the biggest decision point to figure it out. Check trustworthiness by asking people to show up on time, do small assignments, hold each other in small groups. Assess trust by noticing if people do what they say they will do.

At first, the speed of trust is very slow. And then, as trust deepens between people, the speed increases. People often assume that moving at the speed of trust means moving slowly all the time, but I've found the opposite to be true. At first, trust and relationship building take time. As we share our stories, work together, uphold our commitments and follow through on our tasks, respond to pressures, and support each other, we begin to move faster because we know what's important, what our skills are, and what our collective magic looks like.

Presence increases trust. Meetings where people aren't actually there, either because they're on devices or literally not consistently in the room or meeting, will have a harder time generating a collective sense of trust, shared purpose, and collective momentum.

Help groups notice that trust is complex, valuable, a practice, available. Not trust in simply who someone is, but what they are rooted in and growing towards. Many of us are in movement work because we are rooted in trauma and want to grow towards something else, something that won't allow or perpetuate that trauma.

Include a trust measuring tool. There's lots of ways to test for trust: the easiest way is to pair people up and give them a prompt of some depth. If they finish quickly, there's very little trust— they're just offering each other bones to satisfy the task. If it's hard to bring their attention back to the collective because they're so engaged in the conversations, give it another breath, there is a higher degree of trust present—they want to unveil to each other, to be known.

Real relationships make it harder to waste each other's time.

Celebrate each other's lives in the room. Sing "Happy Birthday," look at baby pictures, applaud the graduations and divorces, invite the whole person in.

Woes/Buddies

As often as possible, especially in groups that don't know each other, create an infrastructure for intimacy in the space. The deeper those one-to-one connections are, the more resilient the collective space will be.

Woes (WOEs—those Working On Excellence) or Buddies or Homies or Squad or whatever you want to call it—give people partners, people who can hold them through the various ups and downs that will happen in the meeting, gathering. Even if it's a short gathering, taking time to ground and connect with one other person will increase the presence of connectivity in the room.

Setting up pairs is often a good way to start a gathering, especially one that will last more than one day. Let them partner early in the agenda, and then encourage woes connection at breaks, give them space to debrief together at the end of the day. Here are some good questions/prompts for woes to deepen and get to know each other:

A. **Setting up:**
   Name
   Pronouns
   Access needs for this gathering (what does your body, mind, spirit need to be present?)
   What have you heard about your strengths? What are your growing edges, the places where you still have things to learn and practice?
   What are you committed to?
   What are you bringing into this gathering?
   What do you need from this gathering?

B. **Check-in prompts/Deepening:**
   Tell me a love story.
   What are you here to do? (Here on earth, here in this meeting; the scale is up to you.)
   How are you right now?
   How do you want to contribute to this space?
   What brings you joy? Rage? Confusion? Certainty?
   What do you know for sure?
   What do you know you don't know?
   What keeps you from showing your best?
   How can I support you?

C. **Closing Questions:**

What is the furthest vision you can imagine for our success?

What is the best failure you've ever experienced and what did you learn?

What are you proud of bringing to this meeting? How can I celebrate you?

What do you think we accomplished?

Do you want to stay connected after we leave here?[2]

Embodiment and Ritual

"Our crown has already been bought and paid for. All we have to do is wear it."

—James Baldwin

Over the course of 2018–19, the Emergent Strategy Ideation Institute invited people to come together and experiment with how we practice and learn emergent strategy in person, in real time, in our communities. We practiced together in Detroit three times, then in the Twin Cities, New York City, New Orleans, Washington DC, Durham, Oakland, and Puerto Rico. In every room where we brought the emergent strategy elements and principles and gave people space to create experiments to attend to what was most needed in their communities, what emerged was embodiment and ritual. We put our bodies into motion and relationship, and brought our collective attention to the deepest wounds with the intention of healing.

In each room, there were formal healing practitioners, informal healers, spiritual leaders, those who have been anointed on specific paths with god, agnostics and atheists, elders and newbies and babies, organizers, and artists.

---

2. This can feel awkward, but model some options from the front of the room and give people a relatively low-impact place to practice saying, "My life is too full for a longer term connection, but I am so grateful for what we did here" or "I would love to check in in six months to see how we have been doing" or "Let's text daily practice updates forevermore!"

We did not instruct or create this pattern of embodiment and ritual. In our own ways, including altars, rose oil anointing, and emphasizing being bodies in relationship, we seeded or invited whole-body presence. This pattern of community-generated rituals made clear to me that it is already time to decentralize and decolonize the work of embodiment and healing. We have instincts, lineages, memories, and longings that just need permission and space in order to come forward as offers of care and healing for each other.

We need more people, particularly oppressed people, to be able to listen to and understand what our bodies remember, know, long for, and can be.

We need to be able to set up and open sacred space, and to close and break down and clear sacred space. In each community there are those that open, those that close, and those that hold the container. Build teams with this awareness in mind.

Our bodies can help us find our way back into right relationship with each other, with those who have caused us harm and with this home planet we have been pulled away from in a variety of ways. When we can feel the land beneath us as a place to belong to, and the people around us as those we can trust to hold our boundaries and/or hold our changes, we can begin to imagine civilization as a system of belongings instead of a system of exclusionary structures.

Fortunately, we aren't starting from scratch—we all come from lineages and cultures that include ways of feeling and healing. Unfortunately, white supremacy and colonial patterns both historic and present-day mean that many of our ways of knowing aren't uplifted when it comes to holding standards for how embodiment and centering are taught in the U.S. Even when people of color's culture (nonwestern, nonwhite) is the essence of the content (yoga, meditation, martial arts, healing methodologies, history, resources, etc.), we aren't always recognized for our own knowing, expertise, and teachings. How would we live as people who have survived all attempts at erasure, if we realized we already had the crown Baldwin spoke of, we simply had to give ourselves permission to lead, and learn to wear our power comfortably? As opposed to trying to take someone else's crown, or being the most crowned, or settling for the cardboard knock-off crown, or buying into an idea that the crown is unattainable—we simply have to embody ourselves.

I have seen the crown, or what more specifically shows up as the collective power to heal and to change conditions, appear in so many movement rooms. As a facilitator, sometimes I have known what to do with it, and sometimes I have missed the gift because I was still trying to control it all—wielding power takes different muscles than waging war or weaving critical analysis.

It occurs to me that there are key principles of embodiment that are passed down from many of our ancestors, learned through our cultural practices, that can be accessible through a variety of emergent paths—principles that align across many paths. I'm hoping our movements can benefit from a shift towards a deeper breath, a wider center, a more honest story of our path. Here are some keys:

- We feel what we need to heal.
- We all have permission to feel, to heal, and to channel healing to others. Sometimes we need to be told about this permission...not *given* this permission, but reminded it is already there.
- Wholeness already belongs in the world. The body in its wholeness is true. The body has been packaged to us in a controlled form, or as something that is in desperate need of control, managing, fixing, changing, beautifying, shrinking, strengthening. Something else becomes possible when we orient to the body in a spirit of invitation and respect.
- Listen to your body to learn what you need in order to heal yourself and others. The initial messages might be confusing, still distorted by systems of oppression. Keep listening.
- Find teachers who want to build you up, not break you down or make you into them.
- We benefit when we connect embodiment and mindfulness—inhabit the body in its wholeness, inhabit the

intuition or self in its wakefulness. It's a whole system with all kinds of data, and we can actually process so much, so fast. If we awaken, we can trust the process to be more and more aligned with our highest intentions.

- Take responsibility for your change process. Instead of focusing on what you lack, fixing yourself, or the impossible endeavor of eliminating all hurt and harm, keep your attention on what grows your ability to feel.

- Belonging to yourself is a crucial aspect of belonging to life, planet, community.

- Some knowing and feeling can't be spoken.

- Humble yourself to what is,[3] and appreciate that this is what has unfolded so far. Then notice that you have your whole life to shape what's next.[4]

- Understand what you're saying yes to. Look at how you spend your waking hours to get clearer on what you are saying yes to.

- Only teach what you know. You only know what you practice.

- Decolonizing is crucial on a path to healing, and it is life-long work, as the systems we are decolonizing from are high functioning and all around us.

- Center. Fall off of center, get distracted, get hurt, get reactive, get numb, get human. Then recenter.[5]

- Don't let principles of transformation get caught in any institution. Institutions, even those that seem perpetual, or start from a radical root, are not permanent. Our relationship to the earth and to each other is/must be. Keep transforming to stay in right relationship.

- "We need space to transform ourselves vs. changing according to someone else's standards."—Prentis Hemphill

---

3. "The world as it is is miraculous."—Prentis Hemphill, in conversation with amb.
4. "I just want to celebrate your ability to appreciate and respect things as they are, while maintaining a critical awareness of ways they might be different."—Maceo Paisley, in *The Tao of Maceo*.
5. "Practices that re-center us is why culture."—Prentis Hemphill, in conversation with amb.

Another way of saying all of this:

sometimes, watching moonlight on the surface of the water, if i breathe slow and soften my eyes, i see a field thick with flickering fireflies. it is not a field of fireflies, just as such a field of light, in say a midwestern late summer, would never be a moonlit ocean. but what i see and grasp in that moment is that there is something universal about light in darkness, and change. something that, while experienced in wildly different ways, produces in me the same sense of awe, wonder, interconnectedness, curiosity.

this same thing happens in rooms of people trying to create change. sometimes. with soft eyes i can see that we are a constellation, or a circle of ancestors-in-training, or giant golden buddhas, orisha, that we are in the dance battle of capoeira, that we are in a bruce lee rondori, that we are representative of the whole species, that we are a flock of birds avoiding predation.

i also see us as we are, moonlight on water, a field of fireflies, light in darkness. there is something universal about how our bodies create a collective field of possibilities that is greater than its parts, more advanced than our political language allows for, and deeply needed. given the opportunity, our movements create light in the dark, create space for healing, know exactly what they need in order to loosen the knot that's held them stiff and apart. and our work is not to pour out the ocean, pull the tide, conjure the moon, rotate the earth—even though it often feels that massive; we merely have to be willing to sit there, breathing deeply, and seeing what is. let it move in and through us into action. to let the awe, wonder, interconnectedness, and curiosity in, let it lead.

"Problem" Participants and What They Need

We don't want to see participants in our movements and meetings as problems, but when we are trying to reach a collective goal, there are some challenging patterns of behavior that we can notice and move to create solutions for.

As a general best practice, in your facilitation preparation, ask what kind of patterns and problems the group usually runs into. Shape your community agreements to address those patterns as a preemptive move, inviting people to help shape the space with their participation, rather than detract from or disorganize it.

What follows are some key participant types that were named and workshopped in the first series of emergent strategy facilitation trainings in Detroit. Read with a sense of awareness—what kind of participant are you when you aren't the facilitator? What patterns feel familiar? Which have you seen? Are there others not listed here that you can pinpoint and generate solutions for?

Type: Controller/Ego Tripper

- Problematic Qualities:
  - Shadow facilitator.
  - Control freak.
  - I should be doing it.
  - Constantly referring back to their own experience.
  - Wants to jump to the solution they came up with.
  - Manipulative.
  - Can't, or won't, see their own power dynamics.
  - Opts out of things if they aren't in a leadership position.
  - Uses bureaucratic processes to slow down work they aren't interested in.
  - Can also have founder's syndrome, where they created something and can't or won't let go of it. Won't share leadership.
- Solutions:
  - Notice the strengths. Controllers/Ego Trippers can often process information very quickly and can be highly intelligent, charming, compelling leaders. They are generally highly organized, willing to take big risks, think in terms of systems. They can be great fundraisers, and want to make a noticeable impact on the world.
  - Give them something to control: logistics, developing a proposal from the conversation, care,

leadership development, water, note taking, after-meeting entertainment, talent show—give them work to do that lets their offer be seen.

- ○ Invite them to listen more deeply.
- • One on One
- ○ Acknowledge the power dynamics. Let them know you see them as a powerful person in the room.
- ○ If they are trying to take up too much space without intention, invite them to partner with you in growing the power of others in the room. Possibly even task them to engage a few quieter people.
- ○ If they are intentionally or disrespectfully trying to take too much power, let them know you see and feel their effort, and want to know what it is they are trying to accomplish in the space. Remind them that you are here to help the group succeed, and are not in competition with them.

Type: See Me!

- • Problematic Qualities:
- ○ Want to be seen and acknowledged, even if there isn't a particular reason to focus on them in this moment, even if they don't have something concrete to offer, even if they are off topic.
- ○ If privileged, they may speak up a lot to do performative good—meaning they want to be perceived as doing the right thing or having a solid analysis, but their emphasis might be more on getting affirmation than on making necessary contributions and/or building strong connections.
  - ▫ Can show up as white/male/able-bodied/straight/citizen/wealth or other entitlement.
- ○ If less/not privileged, they may perform a loud woker-than-thou energy.
  - ▫ Or turn every slight discomfort into oppression.

- □ Or continue trying to center their personal story in the collective conversation (especially if it is a traumatic story guaranteed to bring them attention).

- Solutions:
  - ○ Notice the strengths. See Me!s are often brave, willing to be in front of a room, have access to resources, will be eager students, can do the work of modern politics, can do the front-facing work of philanthropy, can be catalyzing forces in their communities.
  - ○ Create opportunities to recognize and celebrate participants regularly.
  - ○ Use the privilege circle exercise written up in *Emergent Strategy* to unveil the power dynamics in the room. Let them be part of the group being seen.
  - ○ Set values as a group around who you collectively want to make more visible.
  - ○ Make agreements that understand that oppression is in the room whenever humans are in the room, and the work is to hold it and face it together.
  - ○ Invite See Me!s to guide icebreakers, birthday songs, host the talent show, the closing circle, places where they can bring and direct light.

- One on One
  - ○ Let this participant know that you see their need for attention and want to understand how to satisfy that need in the room. Make the situation more transparent.
  - ○ For more privileged participants, let them know that privilege can be hard to see when we are benefiting from it, and help them see how their privilege is shaping the room.
  - ○ For less/not privileged participants, let them know your job is to uplift and center their voice, that they don't need to struggle for this.
  - ○ If traumatic stories keep taking the center of this person's attention, you can offer to connect them to professional support.

Type: Passive Aggressive

- Problematic Qualities:
  - Conflict averse.
  - Angry about something, or many things.
  - Checks out when there's tension.
  - Disorganizes the space with questions or passive asides, rather than allowing and engaging in direct conflict.
  - Can try to push people away from conflict to get to the "real" work.
  - Can be unsatisfiable.
- Solutions:
  - Notice the strengths. Passive Aggressives are often highly sensitive, and feeling something that actually needs attention in the room. They sometimes hold a complex, systemic analysis of what's going on, and they usually want things to be more peaceful, may even think they are contributing to that. They have an internal sense of order.
  - Invite people into generative conflict through principled struggle from the beginning of the meeting.[6]
  - Invite the room together to generate some community agreements, protocols of the shared space—often the passive aggressive person is someone who saw a need for a guideline or agreement that went unnamed, and is impacted by its absence.
- One on One:
  - Let them know you can see that something is up with them. Passive aggressives often don't realize their frustration is seeping through their tone or words.
  - Offer mediation so they can directly address issues with whoever is sparking their concern.
  - Support them to negotiate boundaries for being in the space with those they feel conflict towards.

---

6. See "What Is Principled Struggle?" in the Black Feminist Wisdom chapter.

Type: Contrarian

- Problematic Qualities:
  - Always looking for and moving towards an argument.
  - Tantrums.
  - You're warned about them disrupting or delaying the meeting.
  - They particularly look for problems or add complications as the group moves towards landing decisions.
  - They are not solution oriented.
- Solutions:
  - Notice the strengths. Contrarians can be motivated by high standards, want to produce thorough work, help the group face critique internally before taking the work to their community/ies, can be warriors when they get oriented towards the right challenge.
  - Invite people into generative conflict through principled struggle from the beginning of the meeting.[7]
  - Make the decision-making process very clear, and have a robust period for debate and argument.
  - Consider actually structuring debate into your agenda.
- One on One:
  - Trust the people. Talk to this person and find out what is at the heart of their resistance. Let the participant know how their participation is impacting the room.
  - Give examples of moments when their contrary nature was not useful for the work of the whole.

---

7. See "What Is Principled Struggle?" in the Black Feminist Wisdom chapter.

Type: Overstimulator

- Problematic Qualities:
  - Super Responder. Doesn't leave time for slower responders to be in conversation.
  - Rambles and goes on a million tangents when they get a chance to speak.
  - Has no intuition for one mic, one person speaking at a time, and they keep jumping in when others speak.
  - Can emotionally jump in on other's experiences.
  - Can have problematic content in the overflowing need to talk.
  - Jokester, often at inappropriate moments.
- Solutions:
  - Notice the strengths. The overstimulator wants to participate! They want to be involved, they are excited by the content, they have a lot to share, and often want to contribute to a positive mood.
  - Set clear agreements on the front end around sharing the mic, one speaker at a time. If needed, use the practice common to many of our ancestors of using a talking item to indicate whose turn it is to speak. In large rooms this can be a literal microphone.
  - Center and ground the room, help everyone get present. Interrupting and rambling can indicate a distorted relationship to time, to the present.
  - Practice dialogue, a method where each speaker is limited to two to three minutes with silence for at least a minute before the next speaker.
  - Set timers in conversations where comments need to be short.
  - Invite the room to take a conversation seriously.
- One on One:
  - Give the participant one-on-one feedback around how they are taking up space in the room.
  - This is also useful if the person says something offensive that doesn't get challenged in the full group.

Sometimes no one knows how to correct a harmful share or joke, so you can help the person see the harmful nature of their sharing and possibly take accountability.

Type: The Leech/No Boundaries

- Problematic Qualities:
  - This participant doesn't have boundaries for themselves—between work and personal life, between areas of work, or the boundaries that support a healthy amount of work.
  - This participant overdraws on your facilitator energy and/or other's energy
  - Burnt out. Falling asleep in the meeting/gathering, short tempered.
  - They often have no tangible capacity.
  - May have a pattern of taking things on and then becoming immediately overwhelmed.
  - Oversharing their personal life.
  - Martyr. Unable to set boundaries between work and rest, play, family, friendships. Expects others to operate without boundaries as well. Unable to grasp the boundaries others are setting between work and personal space.
  - Always finding someone else in the space to organize on behalf of, or interrupting the meeting to speak about who isn't in it.
  - Traumatized by everything.
- Solutions:
  - Notice the strengths. This person is often a hard worker, or at least wants to be seen that way. They usually need strong, deep relationships in order to sustain their work, which can deepen the whole group. The leech can be empathic and just needs tools to manage their feelings and experiences. They

are often givers who haven't learned to also take care of themselves.

- Have a conversation on boundaries with the entire group. Ask them to discuss what boundaries are normal in the group and if there are boundaries that are needed. If there's a culture of no boundaries then it will be extra difficult to get one particular person to hold them.
- Have a conversation on the culture of the group.
  - If necessary, help them to remove a concept of family, because that often leads to recreating troublesome family dynamics.
  - Help them understand that there can be professional intimacy and that they are in professional relationships.
- Be clear on why this particular group has come together.
- If they are right and there is a person or group of people actually missing from the meeting, make a plan with the group to invite, engage, and/or organize them to be at the next gathering.
- Model having great boundaries as a facilitator.
  - Set good boundaries around your time, availability, appropriate conversations.
  - Hold good boundaries related to the power dynamics of the space—don't use substances with the group, don't hook up with them, etc.
- One on One:
  - Ask if they are tired, if they need rest.
  - Ask them how the boundaries in the room feel.
  - Ask them to make a distinction between this container and the rest of their lives.
  - Let them know it feels like they need to shore up their boundaries. Be specific about what you see.

Type: Ism-Embodier

- Problematic Qualities:
  - Anti-Black/POC. Says racist things, stereotypes people in or outside of the room, white supremacist practices related to time management, work standards, and communication.
  - Homophobic. Makes straight assumptions about relationships, disrespects queer/gay relationships in the space.
  - Transphobic. Keeps misgendering people.
  - Ableist. Assumes a norm for physical or mental capacities in the group or in conversation about the world.
  - Nationalist, anti-migrant. Assumes citizen supremacy.
  - Classist. Comes from wealth, disrespects those with less resources.
  - Othering in general, reducing or dismissing people determined in some way as other than a self-fulfilling "norm."
- Solutions:
  - Notice the strengths. This person has shown up in a movement space, or a space with people of other identities to it. This person often speaks honestly, and is transparent about what they don't know, or where they need to grow.
  - Use the privilege circle exercise written up in *Emergent Strategy* to unveil the power dynamics in the room. Let them understand the differences in the room, and who the group is choosing to center.
  - Set a standard for what a brave space will look like.[8]
  - Acknowledge in your agreements that these are our shared current conditions, the water we are swimming in. Commit to collective unlearning. That

8. See "An Invitation to Brave Space" in the Black Feminist Wisdom chapter, p. 80.

calling one person's behavior in is about raising the collective standard of being and working together.

o Intervene on harm in the room in real time.

o Invite people to learn. Some resources I point people to at the time of writing this:

▫ Racial justice groups focused on white people unlearning racist beliefs and behaviors, like the Catalyst Project and Showing Up for Racial Justice (SURJ).

▫ *Outside the XY: Queer, Black and Brown Masculinity*, edited by Morgan Mann Willis

▫ Sins Invalid for issues of ableism and more.

▫ Mijente.net, a site for Latinx and Chicanx people seeking racial, economic, gender, and climate justice.

▫ Resource Generation, a group that organizes eighteen to thirty-five year olds with access to wealth and class privilege.

Type: Not Well and Unaware

• Problematic Qualities:

o Appears to be having a breakdown in the space.

o Oversharing intense, possibly triggering personal information in the space.

o Incoherent.

o Cannot comprehend that other people (in the space and beyond it) are also struggling.

o OR collapses into codependency with anyone else in struggle.

o Snapping on people and then revealing that the cause of the behavior was some mental or physical unwellness.

o Disappearing, unable to explain how they are or what they're doing.

o Using substances during meeting time in ways that negatively impact the group.

- Solutions:
  - Notice the strengths. Often the person who is showing this level of emotional impact is holding emotions for the whole group, or a segment of the group that feels hurt or unheard. This person might have given a lot before getting to this point. This person wants to move towards truth, towards being transparent about their true state of wellbeing and needs.
  - Recommend therapy and healer support![9] Do not try and take this on yourself unless that is an area in which you are experienced and/or licensed.
- One on One
  - Have an honest conversation outside of the space to figure out if participation is actually possible right now. Give them permission to turn towards health needs.
  - Offer options for more sustainable participation if that is possible. One option is to pair them with another participant as a woe or buddy, to support their participation and ensure their needs are getting adequate attention.
  - Ask the person if/how they want their situation shared with the rest of the group.
  - If there is a boundary needed around behavior or substance use, articulate it directly and clearly.

---

9. The National Queer and Trans Therapists of Color Network (NQTTCN) is a great resource.

Facilitating Across Difference

"We do as much, we eat as much, we want as much."

—Sojourner Truth

The presence of difference in this phase of human history, unfortunately, and too often, leads to harm.

Difference is, quite probably, the main thing we need to get comfortable with, and good at, if we hope to survive as a species.

We are an ecosystem, being told we should be a monocrop. We have some inkling that this bad advice is costing us everything, but so far the majority of us are not convinced enough to take urgent action. Facilitating across difference might be the most urgent work we can do right now.

Difference isn't always visible, obvious, named, clear. Working together, deep conversation, meaningful questions—your work is to give the group experiences that help them understand their differences and, where possible, appreciate them.

The obvious differences create assumptions in the room. It's in the best interest of any group if you, as the facilitator, can speak fearlessly to those differences, and the assumptions, values, and possibly the tensions in the room because of these differences.

We too often slot each other into our existing worldviews. This is a moment where we need to recognize that white supremacy and capitalism have not only split us from our bodies, but split our bodies and innate healing modes from each other.

Facilitation is most exciting to me when so much is flowing intuitively from all kinds of knowing, without a need to control or correct each other. We accept that there are many rivers of knowledge, and then there's the sea where we have ended up.

We need to move past the dynamics of just critiquing each other, or white people, men, the rich—not because the systems that undergird their power aren't still causing harm, but because we have more options than just accepting and living inside those hateful constructs, critiquing them while simultaneously giving them all of our attention. We have a choice to see the constructs, reject the centering of those with privilege, and weave our critiques into what we imagine for our next phase of freedom. We have a choice, every day, to live into the liberating worldview, one our bodies already know: we are not constructs, monoliths, or categorizable. We are distinct and interconnected.

It is time to determine/remember what our bodies know. What we can only know together.

We have to work with people as if we believe they can change. Some people can handle being in spaces with people who are resistant to change (refusing to relinquish privilege, oppressive behaviors), some can't. Feel for what you are called to hold, lead, participate in, or avoid.

To be crystal clear: if you don't believe that white/rich/male/able-bodied/privileged people can reach liberation, don't facilitate them, especially not in processes that require growth and change. It will feel like unfair labor for you, and potentially create a punitive experience for the participants.

Also recognize when a space/group needs a chance to heal and gather without their current or historical oppressor(s) in the room, as a stage of a longer-term journey. Caucus work can be very powerful to create room for nuanced, identity-specific processing.

It's easier to sit in critique and rage. It's justified rage—we have been abused, betrayed, killed, culturally destroyed, and continuously/daily disrespected by those who hold power. And yet, our rage without action isn't going to free us from the dynamic. Boundaries and/or belief give us a stronger core of our behavior: boundaries allow us to hold those who wish to harm us at bay long enough for us to heal and begin to make choices not informed by fear or reactivity; our beliefs give us room to articulate our own reasons for existing, reasons not limited to servitude, oppression, or survival, reasons as massive as evolution, peace, joy, abundance, and destiny.

Practices For Interdependent/Decentralized Facilitation

Increase Access in the Room

Every single person in any room you are facilitating has a body. Bodies have needs. The more of those needs you can meet, the more presence you will have from each person in the room. Here are some starting guidelines for increasing collective access in your facilitation:

- Ask participants (and anyone facilitating, providing child-care, or otherwise planning to be physically present) what their physical needs are for the meeting (including body, emotional, and mental health needs). Check in on these during the meeting, as needs change all the time.

- Let people know if and how their needs will be met. Or that you cannot meet those needs.

- If you can't meet the needs, let people know as soon as possible so they have agency over attending, and time to come up with a plan for meeting their needs.

- Create spaces for participants to be in contact with each other and encourage them to work collectively to meet needs where you/the organizers have limitations.

- Book accessible spaces—no stairs, wide doors, all-gender bathrooms on the same floor. If any basic access needs can't be met, let participants know.

- Have food and hydration available for the meeting. Snacks and water for a short meeting, meals (or a meal-length break) if you're doing more than three hours.

  o Snacks should nourish people's bodies and increase energy. Fresh or dried fruit, vegetables, nuts, jerky, dark chocolate, and other sustaining treats.

  o Avoid snacks that give people sugar energy spikes that will drop, or empty food that takes up space on the table but not in the body. Avoid chips, cookies, highly processed snacks, fried foods, and really heavy food.

- Make sure there are chairs available that are comfortable for long periods of sitting (supportive, cushioned, with backs, and an option without arms on the sides—because thick hips don't like to be contained!), and options for sitting on the floor (yoga mats, pillows, blankets). Participants can be invited to bring items.

- Ask people not to wear chemical scents, and coordinate with the meeting space to ensure that they don't use chemical cleaning products.

This is just the beginning of a list that can help bodies be in space together. Each room will have its own needs, and may have differences from these guidelines—there's not a right way here, there's the way that works for the humans in this room, in this moment. Build comfort with sharing needs, and build a felt sense in your group of having needs met.

Care Bears

This is a framework that supports community care. It was seeded at Harriet's Apothecary, grown at the National Network for Abortion Funds, has served Black Organizing for Leadership and Dignity (BOLD), and was present at the Emergent Strategy Immersions. We are grateful to Adaku Utah for the seed, water, sun, and soil of this approach.

In this model, the roles of care are organized by element—earth, air, fire, water. Earth attends to food and beauty, air to cleanliness, fire to time and energy (this might include ice breakers, and/or fun outside the room), and water to water access and flow.

In most rooms I facilitate, we set up a sacred space or altar, and our care teams are responsible for maintaining the altar items holding their element.

How To:

Participants choose a Care Bear Team that demonstrates how they will care for the community during the immersion.

Or you just count the room off into four groups.

Or use the zodiac sign elements to form the groups.

Here are considerations that the facilitation team should engage:

- Be aware of whether people are choosing teams because it's what they are good at or simply socialized to do. Be particularly mindful of women of color taking on the cleaning or feeding roles.
- Invite people to take this role seriously as an invitation to

experiment with what they want to learn about themselves.

- The most critical skill is listening. Listen to your team, and have points throughout the day where representatives of all the teams can come together and share needs, adjustments—listen for the collective care needs and opportunities.

- An iteration learned from BOLD: each day a different team member leads the team. To deepen learning, at the end of the day, that leader can debrief with the team, giving each person room to share feedback on what the leader did well and where they could still grow.

- Encourage teams to reach out for support if needed. This is a collective endeavor.

- Do less talking and more teaching. Ask questions before telling people.

CARE TEAMS

Earth
breakfast / lunch setup
snack setup
earth elements of altar

Air
clear away mess
air elements of altar

Fire
keep us on time
warmth & beauty in space
altar candle

Water
stock water
encourage hydration
keep / clear water altar

Team Names

Fertile Ground

Feather Flight (FiFi)

Fire Keepers
(AKA Hot they
Summer)

Lifespring

With your facilitation team, determine how you want to divide the work amongst the care teams.[10] You might have additional tasks based on the time, space, or culture of the group. Write "Care Bear Roles" on a large piece of paper visible throughout the space. Write up the roles/tasks for each team as beautifully as possible. Refer to the write-up on breaks, at the end of the day, or if a specific area of work is lagging. Here's an example of what you might write up:

- fire: (time and energy)
  - keep energy burning, remind us of passion
  - set up and clean up breakfast
  - be on time
  - keep the candle burning on the altar
- air (cleanliness)
  - keep energy flowing and clear
  - clean up at breaks
  - be on time
  - light incense or burn herbs for clearance at breaks and moments of tension
- earth (food and beauty)
  - set up the space and snacks
  - keep energy grounded and depthful
  - clean up after lunch
  - be on time
  - keep natural elements like rocks and flowers on the altar
- water (water access, flow)
  - keep energy transforming and refreshing
  - clean up at end of the day
  - be on time
  - set up water offering on the altar, switch the water at the end of the day or after a particularly intense session

---

10. Your facilitation team might be a small group of multiple facilitators, or the points of contact at the organization, or the people holding logistics for the meeting—for some meetings I will have a team of ten to twelve people by the end of the gathering.

Interdependent/Decentralized Mediation

Mediation in movement spaces is a practice of trusting people with whom you are in relationship more than you trust the punitive patterns of the state. It is a building block towards an abolitionist future. It is trusting a relationship to recover from harm by going, together, to the roots of the harm.

All of this means mediation is a fundamentally interdependent practice. It is the result of naming an unmet need for safety or accountability, a need to feel heard, to reconnect, to reestablish the terms of the relationship. Mediation asks: how do we maintain and protect our connection?

Mediation may lead to restoration, to a deeper connection. It may lead to no communication or very solid high permanent boundaries. It will lead to clarity about what is possible and what is real.

One of the ways we miss each other is by rushing through the moments that could be the most transformative or clarifying in our relationships, sometimes because we are uncomfortable with our own emotions or the impact of emotions expressed by another. As the mediator, do your best to seek moments of clear request, clear offer, clear accountability/apology. Highlight and slow down these moments. Notice if the conversation feels like a trial, like they are building cases against each other instead of listening. Slow the conversation down from frantic accusation and defense to a pace at which everyone can express and be understood. Some helpful questions you might ask could include:

- Do you understand what they just said? What did you hear?
- That sounded like a request/offer/apology. Can you say it one more time?
- Can you respond to that request/offer?
- Can you take in that accountability/apology?

Agreeing to be Here Together

Agreements are necessary, they form the riverbanks of the conversation you will have. Agreements help people attend to the common space into which they will pour their offers and needs, and from which they will hopefully be sated. Here are a few agreements I use regularly in facilitation and mediation, along with the thinking that feeds each agreement:

- **Assume good intentions, but attend to impact.**
  - It is actually rare, particularly in a movement context, that people consciously intend to harm each other.
  - Most people want to be seen in their good intentions, their kindness, their emotional intelligence.
  - We will ignore our own shadow-side motivations, sometimes even in the privacy of our minds.
  - One of the first things people say in response to hearing that they caused harm is, "I didn't mean to…," which doesn't alleviate the harm. There is no way to actually know what the person intended.
  - Attending to impact allows people to set intentions to the side and address that which has had impact. What was spoken? What was done? What decisions were made? What was overlooked? What was felt? What is needed?
- **Engage tension, don't indulge drama.**
  - This lesson comes from my years as a doula, watching the journey by which life moves into this world. The tension is inevitable, it is a sign of opening, making way for the future. Life can only come through an opening.
  - Where there is pain, change, grief, effort, exhaustion, and particularly where the work isn't and perhaps can't be equally distributed, drama ensues. Drama is also pretty inevitable in the work to free ourselves from social

constructs that have rooted in our thoughts and behaviors. The tension needs to be engaged, worked with, and ultimately released to reach the next shape or form. The drama needs to be addressed, contained, navigated, cleared.

○ In mediation, tension means that there are multiple people who are alive and care—about themselves, each other, the dynamic, a shared community. Where there is no tension, there is usually apathy, absence, or a dead connection.

○ Tension can peak just before it breaks. Do not be afraid to notice the tension aloud, sometimes this will give people permission to name where the tension is rooting in them—is it that they don't feel heard, understood, or respected? Feel angry with the choices the other person made? Don't feel the other person is being honest? Are scared to be honest themselves? Are scared for the relationship to change? Tension is a communication.

- **Social media is not a space for mediation or conflict. Not in a relationship that is changing or falling apart. No social media about the process while in the process.**

○ Don't organize against each other unless it is absolutely necessary for community safety.[1]

□ Every mediator is different. This is my guideline for how I will support people. I find that inviting too many people into the conversation, especially indirectly, with only partial/one-sided information, limits what's possible.

- **Agree on basic narrative and shared boundaries around the story of the mediation before sharing it with others.**

○ Remember, the participants don't owe anyone their story.

○ If they are going to share their story, make a plan that assures the dignity of everyone involved.

---

1. A community safety need could include letting people know if one person has escalated to a place of violence to themselves or others, or if someone who keeps repeating harm opts out of a mediation or accountability process.

Transformative Justice/Resilience Facilitation

Brief Thoughts on Transformative Justice and Resilience

Resilience is a way of understanding how we recover from harm, our capacity to bounce back.[1] Trauma and oppression are part of the current reality of our species, but there is wholeness and beauty that comes before, during and after the pain. There is a place in each of us, what Maya Angelou called our "inviolate place," a place we can return to.

We are always more than our trauma—individually, collectively, intergenerationally, ancestrally.

We are socialized, trained, encouraged and given permission to punish each other. Punishment starts very early in most of our lives. Time-outs, spankings, detention, suspension, expulsion, juvenile detention, jail, prison, solitary confinement, death...even when it isn't our politic or intention, we pass on these punitive behaviors to others who cause harm or challenge us. In this way, a cycle of punishment perpetuates.

Your work is to break the cycle of punishment in any room you hold.

Particularly if you believe in abolition, in the end of the prison industrial complex. That kind of abolition is only possible if the

---

1. Just to keep it 100 percent, I have never "bounced" in these moments of recovery. Crawled, yes, regrew.

majority of us are willing to give up the comfort, pleasure, or tolerance of punishing people.

In many of our communities, we are making advances with the use of restorative justice—restoring the conditions that predated the harm. This is particularly moving as a strategy to support our incarcerated communities to navigate the existing prison system and have a way to move back into dignity.

Restoration can be a transformative, healing act in a community. But restoring things back to unjust conditions is not actually resilience, so it is important, whatever language we use, that our aim is to transform the conditions that allow harm. Transformative justice is a way of moving into accountability, deepening relationship, clarifying boundaries, and opening the way for more collective possibilities.

"It is the mind which makes the body."
—Sojourner Truth

You need to be able to feel in order to quickly assess for trust. The apocalypse is always possible, and Octavia Butler taught us that we don't know who we will be in the apocalypse with. Feeling helps us to understand who we are in these meetings with.

If you are uncomfortable with an emotion, it will be harder for the truths that speak with that emotion to move through the room. For example: grief. Many of us are scared of the yawning chasm of grief, so we might find ourselves attempting to contain this massive emotion in insufficient windows of time.[2]

Then there's trauma. As a survivor/facilitator, if people share a trauma in the room, I know they usually want it heard and held, not fixed—it's not fixable. Trauma is the way injustice and imbalance leave their marks—abuses of power, privilege, and resource

---

2. Don't miss Malkia Devich-Cyril's incredible writing about grief in the Black Feminist Wisdom section of this book.

that lead to an imbalance in who holds sorrow, misery, grief, and struggle.

There is a truth here that most people of privilege want to ignore and deny—privilege makes it easier to set down their portion of suffering. Some of it anyway, for a while. They can feign ignorance about the urgent impacts a community is facing, while simultaneously running away from responsibility. Or they can publicly acknowledge the dynamics of power, the stolen land, the whiteness, the truth of being funders, how everyone in leadership is straight, light-skinned, college educated—but beyond the acknowledgment, do nothing to change the unjust conditions.[3] This is often the essence of "mansplaining," "whitesplaining," "wealthsplaining," or equivalent attempt to use a factual argument to show a grasp of shared analysis while avoiding emotional accountability. Because they are not directly impacted by a condition of oppression, they can point at some logical, tangible, small, possibly relevant sticking point, something that allows them to hang back, opt out of any collaborative process or responsibility. Know this: those moves of privilege within movement often compound trauma—offering the same power dynamics, but in a gentler tone.

I believe facilitators can be a front line against this counter-revolutionary arrangement. Making the power dynamics in the room visible allows for the room to then work together to bring justice, equality and shared power into practice, within and without, to counter systemic trauma by turning and facing it.

Identity As/vs. Harm

We spend an immense amount of time on identity. Some of this time is well spent on the front lines of changing how we understand ourselves and each other. And some of this time is wasted, or misdirected, focusing on identity in ways that can keep us from getting work done.

Identity is always with us, fundamental to who and how we are. Oppression and the legacies of trauma caused by the myth

---

3. Much of the impetus around money is still to maintain the status quo, the classist dynamics of U.S. wealth and ownership. People with wealth can get in a pattern of investing in crops that seem harmless to them and never bear fruit for us.

of supremacy are also always with us, as is the violence of identity-based capitalism. But they are not always the appropriate focal point for every group or every meeting.

Structure helps us understand where the right spaces and moments are for deep identity work vs. other necessary work. As facilitators, our job is to help groups we're supporting to understand which structure and focus is appropriate for them, and to balance the internal and external work they need to do.

In some groups, the core work is around identity. The relationships are going deep and working to unlearn the internal and external expressions of oppression, racialized violence, supremacy, and inferiority. These are our cadres, our primary organizing spaces, our political home spaces. Or they are affinity groups that help us feel seen and give us room to be heard so we can return to multi-identity spaces.

Then there are broader coalition spaces, which are often organized around small, precious points of alignment. These are most often not identity-focused spaces, even if identity is a common aspect of what brings us together. For example, in a coalition of people of color organizing against climate catastrophe, the people showing up have the shared experience of battling white supremacy, which will inform their work on climate, but they will not be an effective group if the majority of attention is spent on asserting identity, competing around identity, or reinforcing constructs, and not on actions or policy shifts that change how climate issues play out for people of color. Such spaces are usually framed as issue-based spaces, and can take the form of an organization, network, alliance, or coalition.

Understanding which container you are in and trying to build will help you navigate relationships and time in ways that protect forward momentum. Movements need to keep moving.

Oppression Olympics, the phenomena of naming marginalized identities in a bid to compete for who is facing the worst oppression, most often play out as competitions around things we can't control—eventually the race to the bottom stagnates us. Related, Woke Olympics, where people compete to have the most advanced analysis (and often shows up as white people announcing that they aren't centering themselves, or men performing feminism) won't move us far either. We want to unlearn the instinct to compete with each other when it isn't necessary.

Being clear on which identities are in the space and being transparent around tensions can be healthy and affirming behavior. But not every space can or should serve the same function. There are spaces in which every identity, oppression, and intersection can experience being the central focus, but every space cannot be that for every identity, or even aim for it. Otherwise, the seeds of alignment between people who are still learning each other and learning analysis will not get any air or water, will not grow. The weight of oppression will roll over everything like concrete.

Harnessing identity breakdowns to deepen relationship and move the work—that's movement.

I suspect that we are in our tween era of identity work. We understand that we have distinct identities, that some of us face the burden of multiple oppressions,[4] and that the ideas of supremacy that buttress oppression are ahistorical lies, told to uphold unjust authority. We understand that it is crucial to our survival that we attend to who we are and what shaped us.

But emotionally, too often, we use the presence of identity and inevitable identity-based harm to storm away from the table, slam our door, and rage-tweet, rather than staying involved in the collective work. It's become too easy to use identity-based harm to stop a process, especially when we don't quite know how to move the process forward. When in doubt, focus on an -ism in the room…there's always one there.

As facilitators, we must help people create agreements that account for difference and the traumatic legacy of oppression in the room. Even though we appear to be individuals in a room, we are also systems in motion, and sometimes socialized harm can speak through certain bodies in the room. Invite people to practice aiming beyond those trained behaviors, and to quickly recover if socialized harm uses their mouths to move in the space. You can even create structured apologies for people who don't know

---

4.   Read *On Intersectionality*, by Kimberlé Crenshaw.

yet how to make them: "I am aware that [insert oppression: homophobia, transphobia, racism, ableism, etc.] just used me to move in this space. I am sorry for the harm I caused. I will keep learning why that happened, so that I don't repeat this harm."

Continue aiming for right relationship. Aim to create containers that account for the reality of injustice, that unveil power dynamics and name oppression, but reach beyond those immature phases of human development to allow complex, dynamic, and healing relationships.

Practices For Transformative Justice/Resilient Facilitation

Identify places and practices that **increase your resilience,** your sense of wholeness, belonging, safety. Bring items of resilience with you into any space you are going to facilitate.

Track fragility and risk in the room. In rooms that are fragile, the participants feel timid, scared to take a risk, scared to be honest, scared to be vulnerable. A fragile room can look hardened, cynical, or checked out. Or it can look like intensely over-processing individual needs in ways that don't build a collective center or focus.

The level of risk people can take—to be honest, vulnerable, open, direct, to think new thoughts and generate revolutionary ideas—decreases in a fragile room. We want rooms where our participants learn that emotions, honest communication, and generative conflict are signs of strength, and the resulting community strength is worth the individual and collective risks.

One practice I have begun using for multi-day gatherings is a risk spectrum. I ask people to reflect on how they have shown up in the meeting so far. On one end of the spectrum is "low risk," meaning that they have shown up in the ways that feel most familiar, the ways they always show up. On the other end is high risk, meaning that they have risked showing up differently, in ways that took courage or unveiling. Remind people that the level of risk they take is up to them, but that there is a choice available, to show up as they most want to show up, to participate in ways that most deeply align with their vision for community.

Practice transformative justice in your closest relationships. Choose patience, communication, mediation, curiosity, boundaries, and uprooting harm over cancellation, public humiliation, ghosting people, or other methods of disposing of people. The more you practice it personally, the more you will be able to support others through it politically and collectively.

In *Emergent Strategy* there is a **privilege circle**, which is a remix of the privilege walk exercise. Everyone starts in one big circle around the room, shoulder to shoulder. For each experience of privilege, you take a step back from the center. For each experience of scarcity and oppression, you take a step forward towards the center. After a while you have a shape in which those most impacted by oppression stand at the center of the room's focus, and those with the most privilege are on the edges of the space. Those in the center are those whose lead we should be following—they know the truth of oppressive impact and they know the brilliance of survival against numerous odds. Sometimes I actually create a visual of the privilege circle turning on its side in my mind, the center extending forward like the pointy head of an arrow.

"One theory of solidarity asks who is impacted and should actually be leading? How do we put our attention and resources behind them?" Alessandra Orofino, an organizer with Nossas in Brazil, shared this at an Obama fellows gathering.

Transformative Justice/Resilience Mediation

Kitchen Table Mediation

Abolition happens at the scale of relationships.[1] The kind of intimate mediation I discuss here is an offering toward abolition. It is an invitation to release the vengeful and/or petty energy that can derail communities, or at least not let it lead. How many of us won't even attempt forgiveness or mediation, but still claim to be abolitionist?

There is work that is bigger than any of us. There is work that has been unfolding for as long as our ancestors can remember.

Black liberation is the particular thread of ancestral work that flows through my many callings—I am accountable to my ancestors and to future generations for weaving my contributions into the tapestry of Black liberation.[2] Each one of you is also responsible to a lineage, or several, larger than you; a calling that is using

---

1. It's important to note that formal transformative justice processes, where someone has caused harm and is being called into accountability, are a different task. They are usually more intense and deeper processes than those that a kitchen table mediation can or should hold. They often involve multiple support people, holding a harm that would otherwise involve the state, and possibly result in prison. For more on transformative justice, check out *Fumbling Towards Repair* by Mariame Kaba and Shira Hassan, or *Beyond Survival: Strategies and Stories from the Transformative Justice Movement* by Ejeris Dixon and Leah Lakshmi Piepzna-Samarasinha.

2. "The mandate for Black people in this time is to avenge the suffering of our ancestors, earn the respect of future generations, and be transformed in the service of the work." —Mary Hooks, Southerners on New Ground (SONG).

your brilliance, light, and lessons to forward our species. That is the foundational premise of my approach to mediation.

We are not sitting at the kitchen table just responsible to ourselves and our emotions, though each of us do matter, and our personal experiences of justice and liberation do matter. We are responsible for harnessing the creative potential of the conflict—can this be used to deepen our connection to each other? To increase our authenticity? To deepen our commitment to movement? Or to learn something that is crucial for us and our comrades?

Sometimes the lesson is that we need boundaries, or different boundaries than we have. Sometimes the lesson is that we need clearer or more honest communication. Sometimes we need to just slow way down, to really hear each other, to apologize, to renegotiate the terms of the relationship.

The mediator's job is to find out what is really needed to resolve the conflict.

Below are some overall guidelines to kitchen table mediation:

- **Identify the need.**
  - If someone requests mediation support, ask them why they think the conversation needs mediation and what they are hoping for as outcomes.
  - Have that same intake conversation with the other person or people invited into mediation.
  - Mediation often occurs when a conflict is deeper than surface level, not quickly resolved. Mediation can be needed because one person is truly not seeing their impact, or there's been a murky misunderstanding—a mediated conversation is rarely one that works well in a group setting or with an audience.
- **As I said in "Nonlinear/Iterative Mediation" above, you should create the best conditions you can. Flip back to those pages for some more tips on what makes for ideal mediation conditions. I am a big fan of kitchen tables, living rooms, backyards, fire pits, spaces where you could imagine building relationship, laughter, nourishment and connection.**

- **Set Up the Time.**
  - Plan the mediation in bite-size chunks—aim for an hour at a time. Let participants know there is a container of time so they can drop into what they really need to share and what will satisfy them.
  - As the mediator, have a clear sense of what both/all parties want from the session(s).[3]
  - Open with some framing—what is larger than ourselves that we are accountable to? Community, politic, organization, beliefs, value? Refer to this greater thing if folks get too caught up in just their own story/needs. Remind people that their wellbeing is a part of those greater things if they start to lose themselves completely in a collective worldview. Balance, balance, balance.
- **Set up agreements.[4]**
- **Mediate. There are many ways to hold a mediated conversation. Your role as mediator is primarily to make more room for the participants to hear each other. Here are some of my guidelines for how I move through mediated conversations:**
  - Ask each person to enter the conversation with some opening remarks—"What brought you here? What are you hoping to get from this?"
  - Notice if the participants are speaking incoherently, repeatedly moving off in tangents—tangents are a way of looping around the feeling, a way of avoiding the tension.
  - Make use of breath and space.
  - Make sure people are actually hearing each other. Ask them to repeat back what they heard verbatim, or ask what they understand based on what they've just heard.
  - Seek moments of clear request, clear offer, clear accountability/apology. Highlight and slow down these moments.
    - Hopeful questions:

---

3. See more in "Intentional Adaptation Mediation."
4. See more in "Interdependent/Decentralized Mediation."

- Was that an apology or offer of accountability?
- Do you have a response to that apology? Does it satisfy your needs?
- What would help with closure around this conflict?

○ If you need to see the true dynamic more clearly, ask the participants to unpack an ongoing or recent argument. Notice everything you can about their bodies, energy. Content matters, but the bodies will unveil even more of the patterns, the needs, the disrespect and distraction.

○ Notice if they say always, or never. These are signs of hopelessness. When people give up their sense of complexity and nuance, they become less capable of authentic relationships.

○ Notice imbalance, particularly if one person wants to be in the conversation and the other wants to go or be left behind. These are break-up moments, where each move is going to exacerbate the painful dynamic.

○ Help people navigate what often happens in movements—the unplanned collapse of the political and the personal.

○ Look for the moment they realize this isn't a family and may not be able to provide what a family might (or what their family didn't). In order for personal and political needs to be met here, they will have to go much deeper into transformation.

○ The personal/political collapse is why dating within movements can be rough—breaking up shouldn't injure movements, but it often does. Help people take necessary time apart to heal their dynamics, protect the movement.[5]

• **Outcomes**
  ○ Restored relationship
    □ Give people permission to move slowly back into relationship, even if the mediation goes well.
    □ If it feels appropriate, invite the participants to make eye

---

5. For more on this, revisit Transformative Breakups in *Emergent Strategy*.

contact, high five, hug. Let the bodies close the circle of what the conversation has opened.

□ Don't push the participants to create a large number of new agreements to control the future. Let the restoration take root in them, and their new needs will emerge.

□ Let them know that it may not feel good/better right away. Sometimes there is an instant lighter energy, and that's wonderful. But most of us swirl through conversations for a long time after they happen, in our heads. The energy that shaped us into the conflict may have become the most familiar way to relate to each other. If it feels complicated to pivot to a new place, or really release the emotional charge of the tension, tell them to be patient with themselves. Time will reveal if you helped land what needed to land.

- generative somatics offers a useful framework of that after-thinking and after-feeling as backwash. After being honest, especially if we have been holding onto a tension, conflict, or resentment for a long time, our whole system may organize itself into a feeling of shame or embarrassment, a feeling that we were too vulnerable or harsh or a million other things. That tendency to shame ourselves is backwash, and it's often trying to pull people back into a familiar shape. Even if it is no longer needed, that shame was trying to protect us. As a mediator, I sometimes let people know they can text me if they start to feel ashamed or self-doubt about how they showed up in the conversation. It can help to have someone affirm your right to show up, be messy, emotional, and authentic in a world that is constantly encouraging our self-censorship and editing.

○ Boundaries

□ Prentis Hemphill teaches us that "Boundaries are the distance I wish I can love you and me simultaneously." I love this wisdom because it allows us to recognize that boundaries are an act of love, and that even with strong boundaries in place, even if we don't see or speak to each other, we are all still connected. If we set intentional boundaries, it allows us to be connected intentionally, honoring the distance needed for love to fill the space between us.

- A lot of the work of mediation is clarifying needs and generating the boundaries that will allow healing to settle between the two (or more) parties.

- Give people permission to be honest and to walk away. Usually people know when that's what they need, but no one teaches us to do this gracefully.

- Some boundaries are temporary. They'll be done when both/all parties no longer need them. You can create check-in dates—in six months, one year, whatever is appropriate to the participants. "Let's see if this is still needed down the road."

- Some boundaries are forever. Often after extreme manipulation, dishonesty, or harm that was/is ongoing, the work is to acknowledge where the connection is a toxic combination, and set up permanent boundaries.

- People and conditions change! That doesn't mean this dynamic will evolve in your lifetimes. Acknowledge change is constant, and still give permission for boundaries.

- If you're mediating between coworkers or members of an ongoing group, set up a protocol for transparency with other people at the workplace or other members of the group. That doesn't mean telling them everything, but identifying the essence of your agreements and practices that might impact others you work with.

Creating More Possibilities Facilitation

Brief Thoughts On Creating More Possibilities

Always be able to take a breath, that's how you know you are not moving too fast.

Use breath to cultivate patience in yourself and in the group. Values get lost in haste.

Help the group to identify the priority conversations that need to happen. Most of the time, groups are trying to do more than can be done in the time allotted, so none of it can be done well.

Priority conversations are ones where the people in the room can take action afterwards to move towards their shared goals. These conversations may be politically clarifying or logistically tangible or emotionally revealing—or all of the above.

Conversations that keep going around in loops or stagnating are conversations that the group is either not interested in, or not ready to have. Sometimes it means that there is an unnamed political difference playing out just under the surface, or behind the scenes. Sometimes it means there is intentional fuckery afoot—an antagonist, a backseat organizer, or some similar power play.

Negative or positive attention is like cold rain or warm rain, it all waters the seed. It is amusing and alarming how often we are surprised when we give our negative attention to a person or organization and then they/it wins—the election, the grant, the debate of public opinion. Facilitate as often as you can towards positive attention: what is needed? What is actionable? What is a solution we can experiment with? What you pay attention to grows—if your group can only focus on critique and deconstruction, they will grow that energy until they only know how to critique each other. Bring your group's attention to solutions, alignment, and what is possible in this moment.

In a coalition/alliance space, possibilities can get truncated because core values are either not aligned or are being actively transgressed. People should not be asked to contort to a breaking point in order to maintain an alliance.

Make room for trainings or skill shares in aspects of the group's core values or identities that must be respected in order for the group to continue working together. For instance, don't facilitate a transphobic space for the sake of alliance—let training and skill sharing get people up to speed on how a just and equitable standard will be held.

If the time is too tight, prioritize. What is for now, and what can be placed in a future conversation?

Create more possibilities for the roles people can play to contribute to the work. Organizers are very necessary—and that isn't, and can't be, the only role in movement. Create more pathways into movement by helping people understand their skills, passions, and best contributions. We need great administrative thinkers, logistics queens, narrative/storytellers, healers, financially minded people, resource generators, educators, farmers, artists, writers, doulas of life and death, people who are great with children, and on and on. In the long run, we want all kinds of people with all kinds of jobs to see themselves as movement workers.

Facilitation Flow

Facilitators should have an internal sense of the flow that they are supporting groups to move through, and what they as facilitators are bringing to the table.

Here's my general facilitation flow, as an image, and as a set of beliefs. This flow speaks to the overarching life cycle of an organization, group, coalition, or network. What happens in a given session is determined by where they are in their organizational life cycle. What is possible in a meeting is determined by these larger arcs of change as much as it is shaped by the goals and participants in that particular session. Sometimes all of the focus is on getting the structures in place, sometimes it's about identifying a moment of great conflict, or a moment of splitting or sunsetting.

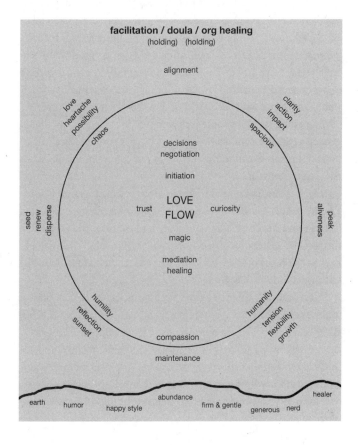

The energy of seeding something new, and renewing something that exists is similar—dark, beautiful, fertile energy.

New projects begin because we love our people, because something breaks our collective hearts, or because we can see the possibility for growth for ourselves, our communities, or our species.

In the foundational period of an organization there is chaos. Accepting that the chaos is normal and natural will help us claim our creative potential in it. Accepting the chaos allows us to stop demanding impossible things from each other (such as clear prophetic answers on how everything in the future is going to work) and shift into inviting each other into co-creation of futures that work for us.

Our work as facilitators is to listen for the points of **alignment** that will lead to internal spaciousness and external expressions of clarity, taking action, and making impact. Holding groups through these stages, we can be organizational doulas, helping the group feel for their own power, knowing, and opening. We are supporting them to make foundational decisions, and negotiating how their values are shared with each other and in the structure and practices of their work. As all of these pieces come into play, and alignment becomes real, the organization reaches its first period of peak aliveness. It all feels worth it, the impact to the community is palpable, the purpose is clear.

During this first period of group growth, time together is feeding the center, the heart of the group. In my facilitation flow, I'm feeding love into the center and drawing love from the center. I'm focused on generating trust, intuition, magic, and curiosity. As long as the heart of the work is full of those ingredients, I trust the lessons we will learn together.

Once the alignment is alive, organizations enter a period of **maintenance**. Internally, group members start to really see and feel their humanity, their complexity, their contradictions. Externally this can show up as tension (between different organizations or internal tension that shows up by slowing down the organization's work), flexibility (being able to meet a number of different needs), and growth (growing in numbers but also in narrative, in accomplishments to celebrate).

This is often the first time the organization needs some sort of internal mediation or organizational healing. In this period facilitators and leaders want to be in a commitment to generating compassion in the organization, not letting people fall into a culture of gossip, complaint, or judgment.

The healthiest organizations move into humility here—the humility to learn these big lessons and either reflect and find the adaptations to make, or recognize that it's time to sunset the organization, let it dissolve and disperse into other movement projects.

One of our facilitation roles is to help groups remember that they are not the first humans to try to change the world, have a vision, wrestle with philanthropy, grow, have a financial crisis, have internal conflict, contradiction, and/or combustion, or to end. If groups can grasp that others have tried and experienced all of these things, they can return to curiosity and experimentation.

It's also important to know what's in the soil of you, the facilitator. What are the unique qualities you consistently bring to the ecosystem?

I bring earth energy and ground into the room with me, which includes abundance and generosity, because the earth gives from a plentiful resource. I'm comfortable being myself, bringing my humor, my firm calls into accountability, and my gentle touch to keep groups on track. I dress in ways that make me happy, I'm out as a nerd, and I'm learning to harness the power I have as a healer in any room I facilitate.

Write about who you are and what you bring to any room you enter as a facilitator.

Use Your Magic

Don't be afraid of your magic—use it.

Everyone has magic. Magic is not charisma or performance. (Use these too, if it serves the universe, serves god-is-change.)[1]

Your magic is that which you cannot quite articulate, that which changes what is possible in any room you enter.

---

1. "God is change." Octavia E. Butler, in her *New York Times* bestselling novel *The Parable of the Sower*, asserts that change is the divine constant afoot in the world, and the force that we must learn to partner with and shape. I am beginning to replace "god" with "god-is-change" to speak to this alternate way of understanding the sacred interconnecting force that touches all of us.

Some of you conjure your magic, using elements of the material world to generate the future. You might call yourselves witches, wizards, priests, students—you learn your magic thru teachers who are farther along on the path, through listening or reading, intuition or scholarship. You use your magic to make altars, cast spells, conjure openly, with consent.

Some of you work with illusions. You can create a vision for people that feels palpable and awakens new longings.

Some of you embody a magic—goddesses, gods, ethereal beings, alien, ancestors-walking, bodhisattva, saints, caregivers, whisperers. You may realize what you are through trial and error, trying and failing to be smaller, more normal. Your power is palpable, undeniable, a sun-bright light that won't be hidden from view. You learn to wield your power thru surrender, particularly of limiting internal logic, imposter syndrome and the tools of the disconnected. If you are connected, there is less to figure out, less to analyze. To be a sacred being is to be connected. Your magic is to help everyone connect, to recognize that everyone is a sacred being and that disconnection is intentional, political, and evil. Once you remember this, it is easier to find your contribution. How do you bring back connection?

Some of you are a combination: conjuring goddesses, witchy saints, visionary caregivers. You find the miracle through curiosity. You spend a lifetime learning to combine connection and intention. You save a lot of people, but imagine how many more you could save if each of you realized you're all divine. Part of your work is to remind everyone of their sacred selves. People may call you a leader or healer. You focus on working and learning to achieve what God-perception says is possible to the limited body, to all of these bodies.[2]

Some of you are none of these things. The work of holding space may be harder for you. You may never feel satisfied in this role. While everyone can learn the basics of holding change, that doesn't mean it is a universal calling. Fearless and practiced magic help—magic of time, magic of faith, magic of vision, magic of earth, magic of connection.

---

2.   Disability Justice is a universal awakening.

I'd guess a handful of every hundred people are deeply called to hold change, hold the space in which humans transform. The majority of people need to be in the space held, the space generated in a good process.

This may be controversial, but it's a stance I want to articulate at least once in this book: everyone should have basic facilitation and mediation skills, but only those with some combination of these specific magics should *solely* do facilitation and/or mediation. As we see with singing, writing, dancing, acting, inventing, parenting, we all have different callings, gifts, and magics. I believe facilitation is a skill and a calling, and yes, I believe at its best it is magic.

Questions as Direction

Gather around key questions. Even if the group articulates goals, be clear on the questions they are asking.

Do not answer these questions, but bring the group's attention to them, see what answers they have. Some people can only see answers in the form of actions. Others can only see answers in the form of political articulation, working together to state a political position. Still others can only see answers in the form of positional power—they won't be able to engage in addressing questions until the structure and decision-making dynamics are clear.

Part of your work is to understand what kinds of answers will satisfy this group's questions. You can also help a group by showing when the questions people are trying to answer are wildly divergent.

Some of my favorite key questions:

- Which ancestors do we ask to guide our work?
- What do we want our legacy to be?
- Which organizations do we look up to?
- Is our tendency towards reform or revolution?
- Are we the right we for this work?
- Why us, now?
- What does our community most need right now? And how do we know that?
- What is it that we are uniquely suited to do?

- What if we had unlimited resources?
- What if we can only do one thing as a group?
- Is this a moment for intentional adaptation?
- Are our values alive in this decision?
- What is the next most elegant step?[3]

Find questions you can spend your life answering.

Generating Hope

Some of your main work is helping people change their minds. And helping "keep hope alive." Not a false hope in changes that are never coming, but practiced, informed optimism rooted in tangible changes of behavior, attitude, belief, and motivation.

Find out who the group wants to be, and give them opportunities to become that. Reflect back to them all the ways you see them growing, attending to the smallest shifts like a gardener with a seed just bursting open in her dirt. Encourage people with statements like, "yes, that's right, that's change, there it is. Imagine what we will do further down in that direction!"

A hope that can move a room needs some rooting in what is. Skepticism is part of what is, but so is the attendance and participation of the skeptical. Even if someone comes to the meeting frowning or sucking their teeth in doubt, there is hope in that showing up, in that entering. Don't waste it. Often the grumpiest person in the room is the one with the most tangible vision, or the most need for our efficient and impactful work. I love my apparently hopeless participants, they remind me that it is egregious the amount of radical time we waste in bad process, the amount of community attention capital we squander. Real relationships make it harder to waste each other's time. Real relationships are a building block of hope that can change material conditions.

> "You'll be free or die."
>
> —Harriet Tubman

---

3. This beloved question comes from movement facilitator Gibran Rivera.

Practices for Creating More Possibilities Facilitation

Altar Building

One of the easiest and most guaranteed ways to create more possibilities is to ask for help from beyond the room. I do this by creating an altar.

Altars can do many things. They are a way to focus our energy for manifestation, collective intention, emotional request, and emotional release. They can call in the support of the elements from the natural world, from the spiritual world, from the ancestral world. They can be a space to hold items that are meaningful to us, items that are a physical manifestation of our commitment to the work, to learning, to this life.

Some altars are specifically for honoring and communicating with our ancestors. We offer them nourishment, we put their faces and words on the altar.

A few best practices for altar building:

- Represent the elements on your altar.
  - Fire: A candle, or something forged in fire (a key, a ring, most things made of metal).
  - Water: A cup or bowl of water. Water gathers energy,[4] so dump the water each day and start fresh the next morning.
  - Air: Incense, sage, palo santo, a feather, items that shift or ride the air.[5]
  - Earth: Dirt, wood, leaves, pine cones, stones, crystals.
- Many lineages have guidelines around honoring ancestors in separate spiritual spaces than those in which we honor the living. A simple way to attend to this is not to include any pictures of the living on ancestor altars.

---

4. Study the work of Masaru Emoto.
5. Pay attention to who is in the room and the items you select. You want to use items that are appropriate for your location, lineage, and for the culture of the room. Cultural appropriation happens when you adopt the spiritual or cultural practices of those who have been marginalized or oppressed. Don't let spiritual space be abused as a place of harm.

- If you don't have a personal practice of building and using altars in your own life, don't lead this practice in the room. You can let people know that the option is available to them, that there is room for them to build and create an altar if it aligns with their practices.
- Access Check
  - Make sure you know what is allowed in terms of fire and scent in the space you're gathering—some places have fire codes, or low chemical protocols.
  - Check with participants around the use of scent in the space—even if the building allows it, some people have asthmatic or other negative reactions to burning things in the space.

Visualization

Invite the room to visualize from what is to what is changing. Here are a few short scripts for guided visualizations:

- Visualize yourself as you are changing. See yourself a decade ago, that face, that energy, that doubt, those questions, those friends, that work. How much has changed in this last decade? How have you changed? Now cast into the future another decade. How old will you be? Are you doing the same work? Who is in your life? How have you changed? What is one step you can take today towards those changes?
- Visualize a future where Black lives matter. Where trans lives matter. Where Indigenous lives matter. Where earth life matters. [Insert the lives of those present in the room, and those impacted by those in the room.] Where your life matters.
- Visualize our work here today if we were completely successful. What changes because of our work? What becomes more possible? What is no longer allowed? How does it feel in that world?
- Centering visualizations: I find that the poetics of centering are often invitations to visualize and reshape myself

in a moment. For some people these visualizations drop us into center as we find our way to sensation. Forwards, backwards.[6]

○ Relax into gravity, extend your roots down into the earth. Extend up towards the sky. You are a line of light moving from the center of earth out into the darkness of space, deep knowing to the wide unknown. You are mostly stardust, so this may feel like memory, like something you've done before. Let that starlight be you in your dignity.

○ Visualize us as a circle of redwoods, deeply rooted and growing towards the sun.[7]

---

6. See the practices in the "Intentional Adaptation Facilitation" chapter for more on centering.

7. I first heard this visualization from Nazbah Tom, and it now shows up for me often when I am with a group of history makers.

Creating More Possibilities Mediation

Be willing to introduce the idea of mediation into a room you are facilitating, or community you are holding or participating in. This is one of the first steps we can take to creating more possibilities in our communities. You may have heard of the ideas of power over versus power with—there are those who practice power as a way to be above others, to hold power over them, and those who practice holding power with each other, as peers and co-creators of the present and future. I believe there is also a practice of power under—that we can get comfortable in the role of subservience, subordination, not even imagining that we could be in equitable relationships of power. From this place we wield our power through venting, complaints, and dissatisfaction. Instead of just listening to our comrades take a consistent stance of power under, how can we invite people into held space in order to clear their dissonance?

There is Enough Time. Wherever we practice, time is the most common resource that feels scarce. Time is one of our greatest common practice areas of scarcity. Let people know there is enough time for them, for their feelings and needs to be met, for their future to be shaped.

That time also needs to be real. Schedule a next session. Get people used to the idea that there is enough space in the timeline for their needs to be met, and/or help people find the adequate spaces. Perhaps what they really need is a therapist, from whom they get time for their own work. Help them connect to any of the incredible networks of therapists and healers.[1]

Your nos make the way for your yeses. Remind those you facilitate that they are allowed and encouraged to create boundaries and that practicing those boundaries will give them the most options for where to go from here, because those boundaries allow room for healing and trust building thru shared commitments to honoring each other.

Communicating the outcome of any mediation can help let other people know that mediation itself is always a possibility! If it feels comfortable to both/all parties, which may take some time, let the community know that mediation happened, and that it has helped. This is not required, and it is not a way to measure the success of a mediation process. If it does feel available, let people know mediation helped the people involved. Let's normalize the human need to ask for help!

---

1. Check out BEAM.org for networks specifically for Black, picPOC, queer communities. I also vouch for Talkspace, which really helped me when I was in too much transit for a regular conversation.

A Brief Note on Visibility and Facilitation

I'm not sure you can be famous and facilitate movement spaces.

Now, I'm still not convinced that I qualify as a famous person or celebrity, because I am so thankfully unknown to so much of the world. But within movement spaces my writing has catapulted me to a different level of visibility and influence. And I know that, relative to what I've always experienced as a facilitator, things have changed with my increased visibility in ways I could not have predicted, and would not have chosen. I thought I would always, always be doing mostly this work. Now, it feels less possible to do it in the way I most deeply believe it is meant to be done.

A facilitator is meant to be part of the container, a force in the river. Walls, doors, and windows. Sediment and wave. Not the centerpiece, not the boat.

I probably sound dramatic, but the work is to feel what is happening in the room, and more often in rooms I'm trying to facilitate, I can feel that people are no longer interacting with me as part of the container, as a force in the river. There's a mix of timidity, "I don't mean to fangirl," not wanting me to see the problems, or assumptions about what I believe and how that might influence my choices in holding the group. Most of the time this is positive, and people are loving, even excited for me to be present. But in a growing, undeniable way, I can feel the difference in the space that my presence produces, perturbations across and under the surface—it's not the difference that a facilitating presence should produce.

I can rarely access the privilege of being the neutral facilitator anymore, which shapes what's possible in terms of how much groups will truly allow me to hold.

Our culture is not designed to uplift people outside of a celebrity paradigm, so recognition quickly becomes a (usually brief) positive celebration, and then a joyful (often cyclical) obsessive energy infused with critique and expectations of perfection. It's heartbreaking when a room can't focus on their work because of some misunderstanding of who I am and what drives my work, or an unasked question about me, or some desire to impress me, or just watch me as a young Instagram star instead of a person doing what I've spent two decades learning to do... As I write this, I learn there's grief here for me around how this change has felt at times.

I share this not to evoke pity but to share the lesson, perhaps as a warning, or at least some guidance. If facilitation is the path you want to be on for a long time then be wary of pedestals. Be wary of things that might seem innocent in terms of accolades and attention. Be thoughtful about what you let people hear and see of you.

I think there's two kinds of famous people—those who want to be famous and will do anything to achieve that, and those who accidentally became famous for achieving skill in something they love doing. None of my mentors were "famous" for doing this work, it didn't occur to me to worry about that. This was the work I was meant to do. For a while. Now, too often, I find myself entering in a defensive stance, or trying to deflect overt attention... moves that only detract from what's possible in the room, from the neutrality the people need in order to focus on the work that they are there to do with each other.

I do feel still joy in facilitation, and in certain rooms I feel like people still allow me to do my job. But it would be wrong not to acknowledge it here, that celebrity culture changes the nature of facilitation in ways that don't serve the collective.

My focus now is offering up all I've learned, with the hope that the act of facilitation can be of service to more people than I could ever reach, especially within the limitations of celebrity culture.

Now my work is to grieve what I could do in the realm of

anonymity, and to ensure that anything else I do is of service to the collective. And hopefully for many of you reading, your work is to facilitate, and to enjoy what happens when you're allowed to be a part of the container.

Closing

In some circuitous way you have found your way all the way through this text. You have dropped through the Opening, you have listened to Black feminist wisdom, you have journeyed through the six emergent strategy elements of facilitation and mediation, and here you are.

Thank you so much for engaging in this text, and I hope beyond words that it is of use to your practice as a facilitator, as a holder of the kind of spaces where change is shaped. I want you to know that I do not see this as an end at all, but a beginning. My deepest intention is that you go beyond anything I could imagine in terms of the depth, accountability, creativity, and, most of all, love that you cultivate within movements for social and environmental justice, within communities committed to finding right relationship with each other and the world. I want you to know that I believe in you, I believe that you are just the right person for the task, and I believe that this text will help you to get clearer on what that task is and how to practice it through to greatness.

I am grateful to my family, full of beloveds who hold space for the tender parts of life in different ways and roles. My family and many of my friends share this calling and I learn from each of you. I am grateful to my love Nalo Zidan, who gives me room to take off my facilitator and mediator hats, to give and receive love and care. I am grateful to each facilitator and teacher who has ever held me, taught me, shaped me. I am grateful to the facilitators and teachers who join me in these pages to offer up Black feminist wisdom. I am grateful to my comrades at the Emergent Strategy Ideation Institute—Mia Herndon, Sage Crump, Luis Alejandro, and Melinda Lee—who supported the work while I wrote about what we were learning and doing. I am grateful to Nandi Comer and Jess Pinkham, who make sure I am able to do my job well. I am grateful to everyone who has shown up in movement rooms with me over the years and affirmed what I was doing that worked and grew me when I was not meeting the needs of the people. I am grateful for the spirit workers and healers and doulas who helped me understand that facilitation can include aspects of each of those gifts.

I am grateful for what I have learned so far and what I will continue to learn.